STUDENT LEARNING ASSESSMENT

OPTIONS *and* RESOURCES

Middle States Commission on Higher Education

Published by the

Middle States Commission on Higher Education
3624 Market Street
Philadelphia, PA 19104

Telephone: 215-662-5606
Fax: 215-662-5501

www.msache.org

This publication replaces *Framework for Outcomes Assessment* (1996) and *Outcomes Assessment Plans: Guidelines for Developing Assessment Plans at Colleges and Universities* (1998).

Printed in the United States of America

Contents

List of Figures

Acknowledgements

The Middle States Commission on Higher Education is grateful for the assistance of its Advisory Panel on Student Learning and Assessment for developing the text of this publication, Assessment of Student Learning: Options and Resources. This publication reflects the work of the panel, the Commission and its staff, and some colleagues in higher education.

The Advisory Panel on Student Learning and Assessment
[Positions as of Date Appointed: June 2001]

Dr. Peter J. Gray (Chair), Associate Director, Center for Support of Teaching and Learning, Syracuse University

Dr. Michael J. Dooris, Director, Planning Research & Assessment, The Pennsylvania State University

Dr. Thomas V. Fernandez, Professor of Physics, Nassau Community College

Dr. Bruce Keith, Assistant Dean for Academic Assessment, United States Military Academy

Dr. Armand S. LaPotin, Professor of History and Academic Program Coordinator, SUNY College at Oneonta

Dr. Elizabeth Larsen, Professor, Coordinator of General Education, West Chester University of Pennsylvania

Dr. Jodi H. Levine, Assistant Vice Provost for University Studies, Temple University

Dr. Rosalyn Lindner, Senior Advisor to Provost for Assessment, SUNY College at Buffalo

Dr. Peter J. Miller, Assistant Professor, Department of Physical Therapy, University of the Sciences in Philadelphia

Dr. Paula E. Peinovich, Vice President for Academic Affairs, Excelsior College

Ms. Linda A. Suskie, Director of Assessment, Towson University; Former MSCHE Fellow

Dr. Barbara E. Walvoord, Director, Kaneb Center for Teaching and Learning; Concurrent Professor of English; and Fellow, Institute for Educational Initiatives, University of Notre Dame

Prof. Katrina A. Zalatan, Assistant Professor of Management, Hartwick College

Additional Support Provided by:

Dr. MaryAnn Baenninger, *Editor-in-Chief*; MSCHE Executive Associate Director

Ms. Jean Avnet Morse, *Editor*; MSCHE Executive Director

Mr. Oswald M. T. Ratteray, *Editor*; MSCHE Assistant Director for Constituent Services and Special Programs

Ms. Siobhan Underwood, MSCHE Graduate Fellow and Assistant to the Advisory Panel

Introduction

Colleges and universities have long defined and assessed student learning using course-embedded assessments of student learning, such as tests, papers, projects, as well as standardized or "custom" qualitative and quantitative measures. All of these are valid and valuable assessment tools if used properly.

In order to reach out more effectively to students and to the public, the Middle States Commission on Higher Education revised its accreditation standards, *Characteristics of Excellence in Higher Education: Eligibility Requirements and Standards for Accreditation,* to refine the requirements and recommendations for establishing learning goals and assessing student achievement.

The members also concluded that the process of defining and assessing student learning would assist faculty in their teaching, students in selecting institutions and in managing their own learning, and institutions in planning and supporting students.

This handbook serves as a resource for institutions seeking a bridge between the Commission's standards for accreditation and the practical daily challenges of assessment and continuous improvement.

How Accreditation Helps

It is in the interests of currently enrolled and prospective college students, faculty members, parents, high school teachers and guidance counselors, legislators, employers, and the general public to be informed consumers of higher education.

One function of accreditation is to provide the public with an explanation of the broad scope of higher education and to assure the public that the goals of higher education have been achieved by evaluating each institution within the context of its mission.

One of the means by which the public can understand higher education is through information about the assessment of student learning. As an institutional accreditor, the Middle States Commission on Higher Education, with the support of its institutional members, acts on the judgments of volunteer peer reviewers who certify that institutions assess themselves in all areas, including student learning.

Accreditation Standards

Among the principles that guided the revision of the Commission's standards is greater emphasis on institutional assessment and the assessment of student learning. By complying with the standards, accredited institutions assure the public that they provide quality higher education. **Specifically, the Commission's process demonstrates that institutions identify student learning goals for educational offerings that are appropriate to its higher education mission; that its offerings display appropriate academic content, rigor, and coherence; that its curricula are designed so that students demonstrate college-level proficiency in general education and essential skills, including oral and written communication, scientific and quantitative reasoning, critical analysis and reasoning, technological competence, and information literacy; and that assessment demonstrates that students at graduation have achieved appropriate higher education goals.**

The accreditation standards relating to assessment are intended to foster and cultivate the progress of member institutions. They are not intended to be prescriptive. Each standard stresses the significance of self-study and peer review as a developmental activity. The ways in which individual institutions carry out assessment activities and determine the extent to which their goals for student learning have been met is an institutional prerogative. Because of the diversity of institutional types, missions, and educational practices that characterize the members in the Middle States region, *Characteristics* provides institutions with guidance on how different types of institutions might fulfill each standard.

Characteristics of Excellence in Higher Education reflects this renewed and increased emphasis on institutional assessment and the assessment of student learning in several ways. Each of the 14 standards is accompanied by "fundamental elements" that guide the institution in assessing itself on the standard.

With the increasing use of alternative forms of delivery, including distance learning and asynchronous delivery, a focus on outcomes becomes even more essential. Student learning outcomes form a "common currency" with which one can judge the equivalence and value of various learning experiences.

The standards are organized into two subsections: Institutional Context and Educational Effectiveness. The concluding standards of each of these two subsections require that an institution define, evaluate, and continually refine its overall goals (Standard 7), with special emphasis on goals for student learning (Standard 14): ·

> **Standard 7: The institution has developed and implemented an assessment plan and process that evaluates its overall effectiveness in achieving its mission and goals, its efficiency in the use of its resources, and its effectiveness in assuring that its students and graduates achieve the appropriate learning and other outcomes.**

> **Standard 14: Assessment of student learning demonstrates that the institution's students have knowledge, skills, and competencies consistent with institutional goals and that students at graduation have achieved appropriate higher education goals.**

These standards are mutually supportive, because they recognize the centrality of student learning to institutional effectiveness and stress that the assessment of outcomes should be integrated into the institutional planning process. See Appendix 1 for an expanded description of these standards.

Purpose and Scope of this Handbook

This handbook is intended to clarify principles and methods for setting goals for student learning within the context of institutional mission, for using methods chosen by the institution for evaluating the achievement of these goals, and for using the information gathered to continue to improve student learning. **It is not an expansion of the Standards for Accreditation described in *Characteristics*; it is meant only as a resource.**

Teams that evaluate institutions at the time of their decennial self-studies and evaluators who review institutions' Periodic Review Reports, Follow-up Reports, and Substantive Change proposals will use the standards themselves, rather than this handbook, to assess the institution.

The audience for this handbook includes all stakeholders of a college or university, including faculty, students, staff, administrators, and the general public. It is intended to assist directly those responsible for setting goals for student learning and for evaluating the achievement of those goals.

This handbook describes:

- ❑ How faculty and staff members can define clearly student learning and affective goals appropriate for an institution's mission;

- ❑ Various direct and indirect methods of evaluating student learning and the value and appropriate use of each approach;

- ❑ How student learning can be improved by relating outcomes to the institution's operations and resources; and

- ❑ How traditional methods of teaching and learning can be enhanced to produce clear and useful information about how and what students are learning, both inside and outside the classroom, so that faculty, students, the institution, and the general public can benefit from improvements.

The handbook presents various possible means of meeting the Commission's standards. It describes various contexts and options for assessing student learning, and it provides resources as examples of how institutions *might* approach the assessment of student learning on their campuses. It also discusses some of the many considerations that should be explored before intensive institutional effort is directed at articulating learning goals, choosing means of evaluating the accomplishment of those goals, and crafting an institutional plan for assessment.

Guiding Principles

This handbook serves as a starting point for institutions beginning or enhancing their self-assessment activities, particularly those activities related to student learning.

It is written for faculty, staff, and administrators—those who will actually be leading and conducting assessment efforts on their campuses. Its purpose is not limited to providing a route to achieving accreditation or reaffirmation of accreditation, but rather it is intended as a resource and guidebook for institutional self-reflection, improvement, and achievement of the best possible outcomes for students.

It also can be a resource for those who wish to learn about assessment practice in general: what it is, why it is important, who benefits from it, how it is accomplished, and how accreditation supports assessment.

Six guiding principles serve as the framework for this handbook, and they are relied on throughout the handbook. These principles are adapted from AAHE's principles for good practice in assessing student learning (Astin, 1991) and *Assessment in practice: Putting principles to work on college campuses* (Banta, Lund, Black, and Oblander, 1996).

While the recommendations, ideas, resources, and perspectives in this handbook are offered as examples and as flexible models and blueprints, there is no "one size fits all" type of institutional assessment or student outcomes assessment. Thus, the principles presented here should serve as the basis and guiding structure for assessment activities and the resources described in the handbook should serve as possible tools—among many—for achieving institutional goals.

Guiding Principle 1: Existing Culture

Begin by acknowledging the existence of assessment throughout the institution in order to ensure that the assessment plan is grounded in the institutional culture.

Guiding Principle 2: Realistic Plan with Appropriate Investment of Resources

Plans for assessment at the program, school, and institutional levels should be realistic and supported by the appropriate investment of institutional resources.

Guiding Principle 3: Involvement of Faculty and Students

Academic leadership is necessary in order to gain the support and involvement of faculty members, staff, administrators, and students across the institution.

Guiding Principle 4: Clear Goals

Assessment activities should be focused by a set by clear statements of expected student learning (knowledge, skills, and competencies).

Guiding Principle 5: Appropriate Methods

Assessment should involve the systematic and thorough collection of direct and indirect evidence of student learning, at multiple points in time and in various situations, using a variety of qualitative and quantitative evaluation methods that are embedded in courses, programs, and overall institutional processes.

Guiding Principle 6: Useful Data

Data gained through assessment activities should be meaningful. They should be used, first, to enhance student learning at the institutional, program, and course levels; second, in institutional planning and resource allocation; and third, to evaluate periodically the assessment process itself for its comprehensiveness and efficacy.

The guiding principles are intended to help institutions answer the following general questions:

❑ What should our students learn? (Chapter 2)

❑ What are our institutional strengths and challenges for improvement? (Chapters 1 and 2)

❑ How are we currently organized for evaluating learning? (Chapters 3, 4, and 5)

❑ What activities have we conducted to define and evaluate all of our institutional goals, with special emphasis on goals for student learning? (Chapters 3 and 4)

❑ What existing evidence do we have regarding student learning and achievement, and what have we learned from that evidence? (Chapters 3 and 5)

❑ What actions will we take to build on our strengths and to address our weaknesses regarding student learning? (Chapter 5)

The Organization of This Handbook

Readers of this handbook will be approaching the task of evaluating student learning from many vantage points. Some institutions will have existing institution-wide assessment plans that need refinement or adaptation. Other readers will be embarking on cyclic evaluation of their assessment plans at the course, program, or institutional level. Still other readers will be just starting to help their institutions set goals for student learning at the course, program, and institutional level.

In order to address the needs of every institution and every reader, this handbook starts with the development of learning goals and individual assessment strategies, builds to the creation of a written assessment plan, and ends with a chapter on using assessment results.

Even readers from institutions that have an existing plan can benefit from the focus in this handbook on setting learning goals and assessing the related outcomes. The section on planning also should help institutions to assess and refine plans.

Each of the chapters in this handbook focuses on a different component of the assessment process and describes considerations, options, and resources related to that component. The chapters are meant to stand alone or in combination with each other, and the handbook can be valuable to support different approaches. For example, the reader will notice that the chapter on planning appears near the end of the handbook, not at the beginning, where at first glance it might seem logical. This is because planning should not occur in the absence of an understanding of the institutional context and an analysis of ongoing assessment efforts.

Institutions that are currently developing or reviewing a plan for assessing student learning might consider Chapter 4 immediately after having read Chapter 1 and then use the remainder of the handbook as a reference.

MSCHE Website Resources

Each chapter of this handbook includes several print resources and examples to support campus assessment efforts. However, new assessment tools and strategies are being developed constantly, and "best practices" and exemplars of good assessment strategies are changing continually.

The Commission's assessment website, located at www.msache.org/mainstudents.html, provides a venue for regularly updated resources, frequently asked questions, addenda to this handbook, and bibliographies of texts and websites related to assessment. The site is organized in alignment with the handbook, and the reader can search for topics and examples related to the portion of the text that is of interest.

1

Motivating and Involving The Campus Community

The purpose of assessment is to engage a campus community collectively in a systematic and continuing process to create shared learning goals and to enhance learning. Those who have direct instructional and supportive contact with the students and those who lead assessment initiatives are responsible for motivating and involving the rest of the campus community.

The best way to motivate the community is to promote an understanding of the benefits that assessment brings to students, faculty, the institution, and the public. The extent to which learning goals and assessment processes that already exist will form the core of a more clear and integrated assessment process.

Students, of course, want to attend the institution that suits them best. Parents want the best value, or perhaps the "cultural capital," that an institution affords. Parents and students are interested in which institution will provide them with the education that will result in a job, or acceptance to graduate or professional school. Employers are interested in the "product" that a college or university produces.

Faculty members, too, have a vested interest in students being informed about their choice of a college or university to attend. It is much easier, and more enjoyable, for faculty members to teach students who are appropriately prepared for their courses, either through earlier preparation or through foundation courses at the institution.

Partners in Teaching and Learning

All campus members are partners in teaching and learning and have a role in evaluating and enhancing student learning. Those who have direct instructional and supportive contact with students include faculty, library and information literacy professionals, and student support service professionals.

Faculty and Students

Faculty members traditionally have had the primary responsibility for facilitating student learning. They determine what students should learn, both across the curriculum and within individual courses or programs, and how students should demonstrate their learning. Faculty members devise methods of gathering evidence of student learning and collaborate with other faculty members in evaluating student learning in their majors and academic programs. They use this information to create a true partnership of learners with their students and to improve student learning.

Huba and Freed (2000) provide examples of how to develop this partnership and the benefits it offers.

Faculty members, who are trained as disciplinary experts, as scholars, and as researchers, can amplify their skills by exploring further how students learn best.

First-year students arrive at their institutions eager to embark on collecting the credits toward the credential they believe they need to ensure their long-term economic futures. If they are traditional residential students, they also seek to experience college life in its totality. Returning students or continuing education students may have other, even more pragmatic, reasons for attending college. Often, however, neither group has had sufficient prior experience in reflecting on how to learn, evaluating the extent of what they have learned and what they still need to discover, or using their new knowledge and skills.

These faculty and students are partners who find themselves engaged together in the pursuit of knowledge, skills, and affective development. They must cooperate to produce the best learning possible.

Sometimes, however, faculty members engage in this process automatically, without questioning the tacit assumptions underlying their concept of teaching and learning.

For instance, end of semester term papers are regularly assigned as a means of evaluating student learning. Yet the typical term paper assignment is a good illustration of how traditional approaches may not necessarily effectively foster learning.

The paper may be assigned early in the semester, without the requirement of an outline or draft of the paper during the course of the semester. The professor's concept of what an excellent paper should be, including its form, its content, and the process for completing it, may not have been communicated effectively to the student when the paper was assigned. Therefore, the student may not have engaged in a process designed to meet those expectations. Furthermore, the paper may be graded after the semester is officially finished, may contain no comments, and may or may not be returned to the student.

Assessment of student learning is not a means of decreasing the autonomy of faculty members. It is a means of increasing the mutual engagement of faculty members, staff, and students in providing an optimal learning experience.

It is important for committed faculty members and other institutional leaders to focus on the faculty, staff, and student partnership, and to avoid top-down or prescriptive rules for accomplishing assessment. For example, it may be tempting for institutions to pressure faculty members to orient professional programs too heavily towards goals that promote only practical skills. Conversely, the need to define student learning goals might be perceived as a potential threat to academic freedom. Close partnership of faculty, librarians, student affairs professionals, and students in defining learning goals consistent with institutional mission should avoid such extremes.

Library and Information Literacy Professionals

Not all learning occurs in the classroom. Therefore, library and information literacy professionals also have a critical role in the process of enhancing student learning. Together with faculty, students, and other staff members, they can address the full range of learning in a student's college career. Ideally, methods of facilitating student learning should exist in other divisions of an institution or should be integrated into coursework. A focus on information literacy is an important component in achieving this objective, especially if it is integrated into curricular and co-curricular facets of the institution.

The information literacy paradigm consists of five skills for learners (Association of College and Research Libraries, 2000):

- ❏ Determining the nature and extent of needed information;

- ❏ Accessing information effectively and efficiently;

- ❏ Evaluating critically the sources and content of the information being sought, and incorporating selected information in the learner's knowledge base and value system;

- ❏ Using information effectively to accomplish a specific purpose; and

- ❏ Understanding the economic, legal, and social issues surrounding the use of information and information technology, as well as observing laws, regulations, and institutional policies related to the access and use of information.

The principles of information literacy are invoked any time a student attempts to learn anything in any discipline. To the extent that the expected learning involves the use of resources available in or through the library, librarians and faculty share responsibility for various aspects of the process for teaching information literacy.

The subject of information literacy is explained more fully in a separate Commission publication of guidelines on information literacy (Middle States Commission on Higher Education, 2003).

Student Support Service Professionals

Those who administer services such as residential life, advising, career development, learning support, service learning, and financial aid are partners with faculty members and students in developing outcomes and assessing student learning. For example, student development personnel help students to develop their own ethical values and to achieve the institution's goal of graduating students who are responsible citizens in a multicultural society.

Leading Assessment Initiatives

Effective leadership is necessary to create a culture that values student learning assessment within the institutional context.

Campus Leaders

Leaders should involve all constituencies in understanding how assessment can be helpful, in identifying the learning goals that are most important to the community, in assessing outcomes, and in using the results.

Campus leaders might sponsor faculty-led discussions of the issues and concerns related to assessment, present workshops led by internal or external experts, organize faculty and student forums that provide an overview of assessment on campus, address larger assessment issues, and answer assessment questions.

Faculty and staff members who work with students should have ownership of the assessment process as well as full and continuing administrative support for its implementation. Such support is best gained through the public recognition of faculty and staff members' ongoing efforts and accomplishments in assessing student learning. Clear recognition demonstrates an institution's commitment to a culture that values the enhancement of student learning.

Palomba and Banta (1999) note that one or more leaders should take responsibility for leading the campus-wide assessment process, that resources must be committed, and that the institutional priority of assessment should be explicit. Activities to involve faculty, staff, and students should be sponsored by the academic leadership and, in particular, supported by the chief academic officer.

Appendix 2 lists some self-reflection questions for chief academic officers to help them gauge their own level of commitment to assessment activities and to reflect on how they might enhance the campus climate for assessment. Appendix 3 is a short "quiz" that can be used on campuses to stimulate discussion about assessment. Although the quiz is designed for true or false responses, many of the questions are more ambiguous than they appear in order to generate a dialogue about assessment; it is not a test of assessment knowledge. Explanations of the "correct" answers may be found in Appendix 4.

In addition to campus conversations, the institution's leaders, and particularly the president and the provost, can be partners with faculty to introduce and to establish assessment by adopting the following approaches:

❏ Increase the awareness of assessment on campus, articulate and define assessment issues and priorities, and identify the institution as an environment that supports assessment practices.

❏ Acknowledge assessment activities that already exist and promote fuller participation in assessment activities by facilitating communication and discussion among the institution's members, with the goal of achieving shared responsibility for assessment.

❏ Be a sponsor of assessment who shares leadership in bringing about this change in the campus culture.

❏ Bring participating members into the assessment process by identifying existing coalitions and developing new coalitions, with the goal of opening the process to as many as possible.

❏ Provide funding and other incentives for participation in the assessment process, institutionalizing assessment, and integrating assessment into the faculty and staff roles and rewards process.

❏ Provide a clear charge to an appropriate campus assessment committee responsible for communicating expectations for assessment.

Institutional Context

The institutional context is grounded in the institution's mission, and it is shaped by the institutional culture.

Mission. An institution's mission, at both broad and specific levels, serves as the context within which to assess student learning, and it is important that mission serves as the backdrop for assessment efforts at the institutional, program, and course levels. An institution's broad contexts will shape overall goals for student learning and how that learning is demonstrated.

For instance, a comprehensive university in the public sector will have a mission driven in large part by the needs and interests of the state, while a private comprehensive university's mission may focus on the interests of its founders or trustees. In the case of the public university, accountability to the state may include the demonstration of service to the community, success in workforce development, and the ability to keep intellectual resources within the state, in addition to the demonstration that students are liberally educated. Private colleges may have missions that focus solely on the liberal arts.

A comprehensive public sector institution may articulate assessment goals through an emphasis on natural resource management, mining or agronomy programs, characteristic of that state's economy.

A private comprehensive university, such as a faith-based institution, may develop assessment goals related to an ecclesiastical mission.

Within the context of its mission and broad context, each college or university will have subsidiary and more specific purposes. Thus, one university might stress the development of civic leadership or technical expertise, and another institution might stress pre-professional development and global citizenry.

The link between mission and the development of goals—in this case, goals for student learning—is clearly expressed in Standard 1 of *Characteristics*, which requires that an "institution's stated goals and objectives, consistent with the aspirations and expectations of higher education, clearly specify how the institution will fulfill its mission." For example, training excellent teachers or insightful managers may express one institution's mission, while training academic scholars and researchers are desired goals for another institution.

Failure to clarify the institution's goals and strengths may result in misallocated resources and confused students and applicants. Students may come to an institution, for instance, with the goal of becoming nurses or biomedical technicians, only to find that the health sciences do not fit well within the institution's mission. The result is that they may find a "disconnect" between the mission and goals of a college or university and the learning outcomes that its students hope to achieve for themselves.

Leaders of institutional assessment initiatives, then, should refer back constantly to the institutional mission and should articulate to faculty, administrators, board members, and donors the fundamental importance of designing learning goals that are consistent with the institutional mission in order to serve both their students and faculty.

Institutional Culture. As an institution begins to plan for assessment, it is important that it consider the particular aspects of institutional culture that might affect the form and process of assessment practice on its campus. Respect for how consensus is achieved and recognition of existing structures, both official and unofficial, will pave the way for reaching the ultimate goal of improving student learning. Following are some questions that leaders or potential leaders of campus assessment initiatives can ask themselves as they embark on new or changed assessment activities:

- ❏ What is the quality of communication on campus? Can it be improved before implementing an assessment plan?

- ❏ How is decision-making handled on campus, both formally, and informally?

- ❏ What is the level of trust on campus? If trust is a problem, how can it be earned?

- ❏ What person or persons on campus are perceived to hold unofficial power? How can those persons be convinced of the benefits of assessment? How can they serve as sources of support for assessment initiatives?

- ❏ What is the system of apportioning resources on campus? If there are concerns about equity of resource distribution (or perceived concerns), can they be addressed before implementing an assessment plan?

- ❏ What is the process by which curricula and programs are approved and revised? Does the process present any impediments to assessment, and can it be improved or streamlined?

- ❏ Are there collective bargaining agreements, union-wide or local, which could either support or impede assessment practices? For example, are union funds available to support faculty development that could be used for assessment? Do union rules restrict "official" work during the summer?

Leaders of assessment on campus should consider these and other factors that could influence the institution's ability to do assessment well. If the campus culture is not functioning in a manner that is likely to be supportive of assessment, it would be useful to take steps to "heal" the culture before instituting large-scale assessment initiatives. Schein (1996) offers some excellent advice on assessing campus culture and suggests that it may be beneficial to an institution to enlist the advice of an external consultant. A consultant can review and describe the campus culture, bring objectivity to the review, and offer a fresh perspective. This consultant could work with the chief academic officer or other campus leader to articulate the underlying assumptions of the culture, reveal any "surprises" lurking beneath the surface, and devise strategies for change.

2

Learning Goals

Goals for student learning are the foundation of meaningful assessment. Statements of desired student outcomes can be derived through a variety of effective methods at the institutional, program, and course levels. This chapter describes the benefits of having clearly articulated learning goals, explores the characteristics of learning goal statements, and provides resources for implementing participatory processes for developing goals.

Benefits of Clearly Articulated Learning Goals

Clearly articulated statements of what each institution expects its students to learn at the course, program, and institutional levels are important to students, faculty, staff, the institution, and the public for many reasons.

Benefits for Students

Statements of student learning goals benefit students because they:

- ❏ Explain the sometimes "hidden agenda" (e.g., the expectation that students analyze relationships between causes and effects, rather than simply learn substantive material)
- ❏ Prioritize which goals are most important
- ❏ Provide assurance that a student has not "missed" an important goal

- ❏ Help students to understand the nature of skills acquired for use in other contexts—during and after college

Benefits for Faculty and Staff

Statements of student learning goals benefit faculty and staff because they:

- ❏ Identify what to teach, including discipline-specific knowledge and skills, as well as the discipline's perspective and values
- ❏ Provide structure for co-curricular programs
- ❏ Determine what will be evaluated at the conclusion of the course or program
- ❏ Ensure that skills that should be taught throughout the curriculum actually are included in instruction and evaluation of specific courses

Benefits to the Institution

Statements of student learning goals benefit the institution because they:

- ❏ Publicize to the institution's constituents evidence that it can demonstrate the accomplishment of clearly-defined student learning goals
- ❏ Ensure that goals the institution itself values are assessed, rather than those used by external assessors (e.g., sophisticated analytical math skills versus minimal national competency levels)

- ❑ Ensure that student learning outcomes are suited to the mission of the institution

- ❑ Ensure that core institutional values (e.g., professional career development and approaches of different cultural perspectives) are sufficiently incorporated

- ❑ Ensure that general education skills, such as proficiency in oral and written communication, the ability to think critically and analytically, and the ability to be effective decision-makers and problem-solvers are included in programmatic plans

- ❑ Ensure that the personal growth and affective development of students are addressed

- ❑ Focus attention on the use of direct methods of assessing student learning, supported by meaningful indirect methods, instead of potentially less meaningful indirect measures often used by:

  - external assessors (e.g., graduation rates, cost efficiency, etc.)

  - internal assessors (e.g., student evaluations of faculty)

Benefits for the Public

Statements of student learning goals benefit the public because they:

- ❑ Enable students to choose an institution based on a particular mission

- ❑ Satisfy accountability needs of legislators, funding agencies, and others

- ❑ Help the public to understand more clearly what an institution seeks to accomplish

Relationship among Learning Goals At All Levels

Before developing or revising learning goals institution-wide, it is important to consider the relationship among learning goals at the institutional, program, and course levels. In addition, different institutions might develop

goals and assess them at varying levels, depending on the needs of the institution.

Learning goals at the institutional, program, and course levels

Students learn specific content and skills in each course. In aggregate, those courses, together with other program experiences such as academic advising, internships, and faculty-directed research by students, should result in the desired student outcomes at the program level. Similarly, goals at the program level combine with general education goals, extra- and co-curricular goals, information literacy goals, and other goals (for example, ethical and civil leadership goals) to create institutional goals. In other words, goals at the institution, program, and course (or activity) levels are interconnected, complimentary, and reciprocal.

Institutions differ in the way that they characterize the relationship between general education goals and institutional goals. In one model, the institution develops a set of overall institutional learning goals stemming from its mission; these goals serve as the super-ordinate (highest level) goals from which program and course level goals flow. In this format, general education goals are essentially programmatic goals; that is, the general education program is one of the programs whose goals contribute to the achievement of overall institutional goals.

In another model, the institution adopts general education goals as overall institutional goals. In this approach, academic and co-curricular program goals would contribute to the achievement of the umbrella-like general education goals, which are essentially institutional goals.

Standard 14 of *Characteristics*, the Assessment of Student Learning, includes language that is most similar to the first model presented above—that is, it describes the assessment of student learning at the institutional, program, and course levels. Standard 12, General Education, also includes its own "fundamental element" related to the assessment of general education.

The Commission, however, is not concerned with the language that an institution uses to describe various levels of learning goals, nor is it concerned with the specific type of hierarchical structure an institution adopts when defining its goals. It is concerned that the institution develops a coherent set of goals, that those goals stem from the institutional mission, and that goals at the subordinate levels contribute to the attainment of goals at the higher levels. The way in which a particular institution defines general education goals relative to institutional goals depends on the institution's mission (e.g., a specialized institution is unlikely to adopt general education goals as institutional goals). It also depends on how the general education program is structured (e.g., Is it "modular" or are its goals met in part through the major? Are some of its goals met through student affairs programs?) Finally, developing general education goals depends on the institution's history and culture.

Figure 1 and Figure 2 describe levels of learning goals at the institutional, program, and course levels. Although some institutions actually create matrices like these to aid them in formulating goals, this matrix is not presented as a model of how goals should be illustrated but, rather, as an abstraction to help the reader understand the relationships between levels of learning goals.

Institutional and Program Goals. Figure 1 illustrates hypothetical relationships among learning goals or statements of student outcomes at the institutional and program levels. The desired outcomes at the institutional level provide the outline or framework for connecting goals at the program level into a coherent whole.

These illustrations include goals for disciplinary and major programs, general education, and a student-affairs oriented program, such as residence life. Goals from various activities and initiatives contribute to overall student affairs goals. Because student affairs and academic programs both contribute to the overall education of the student, goals from each of these programs work together to fulfill institutional goals.

Program and Course Goals. Figure 2 illustrates how program goals provide a framework for course goals. It presents general education as a program, but one could well imagine the institutional goals cited here as general education goals instead. Notice also that some of the goals for programs

overlap and that not all programs work toward meeting all institutional goals.

Figure 2 depicts the hypothetical relationship between a subset of the program goals presented in Figure 1 and sample goals from courses in each of those programs. Notice, for instance, that one of the goals in the course World Art History, to "identify and analyze major works representing several different cultures," contributes to the general education program goal to "recognize and appreciate artistic and literary contributions of diverse cultures," which in turn contributes to the institutional goal to prepare "global citizens."

At the course level, the faculty member teaching World Art History will have many additional goals. Some will contribute further to the achievement of general education goals, but others may contribute to the achievement of goals for the major in Art History. Because of the interdependence among goals and the course and program levels, it could be impractical, or perhaps impossible, to specify all of the links between goals for each course and for each program in matrices. It is more important to strive for conceptual coherence, ensuring that learning goals at the various levels are understandable, meaningful, and accessible to faculty and students alike.

Flexibility

In Standard 14, the Commission recognizes that institutions will be "flexible in their approach to defining student learning goals at these different levels, such as repeating goals (some general education goals, for example) across programs or defining the goals at the institutional or program level as synthesis of the goals set at the program and course levels."

For instance, an institutional goal for undergraduate students to become proficient in information literacy may be achieved through a combination of the active involvement of faculty in information literacy instruction (see Chapter 1), a first-year introduction to library and learning resources presented by a librarian, required assignments in a general education course, and/or a series of substantial research papers required in the major. The goals for student learning in each of these three situations, when combined, may fulfill the

Figure 1

Relationship between Institutional and Program Goals

Note: **Not all programs are designed meet all institutional goals. Some cells are left blank for illustrative purposes only, not to imply that these goals cannot be met by the programs used in this example.**

Institutional-level Goals	Programs and Program-level Goals				
	General Education	Residence Life	Business	History	Chemistry
Leadership	Function effectively as a team member to produce a scholarly product	Develop leadership skills Apply conflict resolution skills in a living-learning environment	Develop leadership potential in self and others	Analyze historical perspectives on individual and political leadership	
Global Citizens	Recognize and appreciate artistic and literary contributions of diverse cultures Exhibit engaged citizenry and value community service	Develop an appreciation for cultural and ethnic diversity	Value and exhibit comfort with cultural differences in business practices Function effectively as a team member to run a small business	Recognize and value culturally-diverse historical perspectives	Demonstrate an ability to work as a team with a diverse group of students
Technologically Sophisticated Individuals	Use technology effectively to communicate and analyze information		Use technology effectively to communicate and analyze information related to business	Use technology effectively to communicate and analyze information related to history	Use technology effectively to collect, analyze, and display data
Effective Communicators	Write and speak proficiently	Communicate effectively in social situations		Communicate effectively, orally, and in writing about historical topics	Cogently present research data and analyses in written, visual, and oral formats
Critical Thinkers	Distinguish critical from non-critical information		Use critical thinking to analyze business case studies	Critically analyze historical events and trends using scholarly techniques	Apply critical thinking skills to design an experiment that tests an hypothesis Collect, analyze, and interpret data relevant to testing an hypothesis

Figure 2

Relationship between Program and Course Goals

Program	Program Goal	Course or Activity	Course Goal
General Education	Recognize and appreciate artistic and literary contributions of diverse cultures	World Art History	Identify and analyze major works representing several different cultures.
		Caribbean Literature	Demonstrate familiarity with themes and genres of classic and contemporary Caribbean literature.
Residence Life	Apply conflict resolution skills in a living-learning environment	First Year Student Orientation Program	Work effectively as part of a group to analyze and resolve a hypothetical interpersonal conflict.
		Seminar led by resident assistants	Develop a plan, in cooperation with floor-mates, for handling conflicts as they arise.
Business Administration	Function effectively as a team member to run a small business	Introduction to Marketing	Develop a feasible marketing plan for a small business.
		Capstone in Business Administration	Work with a team of students to develop, plan, manage, and market a small business.
History	Communicate orally and in writing about historical topics	Modern American History	Present a cogent oral analysis of one long-term effect of the Cold War.
		Medieval History	Present a cogently-written, critical analysis of gender and class roles in Medieval England.
Chemistry	Collect, analyze, and interpret data relevant to testing an hypothesis	Introductory Chemistry Laboratory	Replicate chemical reactions using appropriate laboratory techniques.
		Introductory Biochemistry	Collect, analyze, and interpret data relevant to an hypothesis supplied by the instructor.

institutional goal. Thus, an institution need not articulate specific means of achieving a particular goal at the institutional level, or assess it at that level, if it has chosen to assess it at the course and program levels.

Learning goals are discussed throughout the remaining three chapters of this handbook. Chapter 3 discusses the means by which the attainment of goals is assessed. Chapter 4 describes the development of an assessment plan and where goals fit into that plan. Chapter 5 focuses on using assessment results and how information about whether or not goals have been attained can be used to adapt curricula and programs.

First Steps Towards Developing Learning Goals

The process of developing learning goals should begin with a "situation audit" or inventory of what exists and which practices have been successful. Practices that are identified will provide information for developing a plan for the assessment of student learning, establishing goals, and identifying assessment measures.

The Situation Audit: Taking an Inventory and Starting with What Already Exists[1]

A basic tenet for evaluating student learning is to begin with successful assessment activities already in place. Whether the objective is to develop learning goals and assessment techniques for an individual course, an entire program, or the institution as a whole, an inventory of what exists provides a strong foundation for later success.

An excellent method of gauging the level of an institution's existing evaluation of student learning is to survey the assessment practices embedded at the course, program, and institutional levels. Peter Ewell has referred to this as a "situation audit"—i.e., an inventory of information already on hand that may provide evidence of student learning. Angelo, Ewell, and Lopez (2001) recommend that

institutions begin assessment by "rounding up information you already have."

Institutional Level. At the institutional level, an audit may be accomplished easily by cataloging the means used to assess the entire student body through the activities of offices of institutional research, student affairs, career services, the library, and information management. Most institutions have existing information from some or all of the following:

❑ Surveys of student satisfaction and engagement that are designed and administered nationally and locally

❑ Alumni career and satisfaction surveys

❑ Tests: standardized and/or locally-created

❑ Statistics, such as placement and retention rates

❑ Program reviews of both academic and support programs

❑ Reports by instructional librarians on information literacy and collaboration with faculty members

Program Level. At many institutions, each department and program institutes evaluations of its students that are independent from those of other departments and programs. The choice of instruments and assessment activities is often idiosyncratic, grounded in the approach that is typical of each discipline. A comprehensive and well-designed institution-wide checklist of possible types of assessment activities may help each department to create an accurate description of its assessment activities.

At the program level, the checklist for assessment activities might include:

❑ Senior capstone theses, papers, individual or group projects, and performances or other presentations

❑ Student portfolios

❑ Student research participation

---

1 This topic is placed here in the section on goals so that it appears early in the book, and it is referenced again in later chapters. Its placement also emphasizes the point that institutions should examine existing learning goals and develop new ones before making decisions about adopting previously-used measures.

- ❏ Departmental student and alumni surveys

- ❏ Standardized tests of subject area or broad skills

- ❏ Reports from student internship supervisors

Additional assessment activities may be suggested by disciplinary accreditors who issue guidelines and standards for intended student learning, required or suggested educational experiences, recommended evaluation methods, and expectations for the use of results.

A survey designed to document assessment practices at the department or program level can assist departments in identifying where there are gaps in the learning goals they are assessing, duplicative teaching efforts, and the usefulness of existing assessment results.

Such an inventory also can offer departments a basis for comparing themselves with other departments, as well as creating an institution-wide resource of where to find advice about instituting assessment on their own campuses. Appendix 5 is an example of such a survey.

Course Level. The commitment of individual faculty and teams of faculty is essential. Reviewing existing course-based assessment practices can help faculty members to reflect on assessment practices that have become routine. A review of course materials can provide useful insights into what students may or may not be learning.

A well-constructed course-level checklist might include:

- ❏ Embedded assessment elements faculty prepare, such as syllabi, curricula, instructional materials and methods, assignments, exams, and quizzes

- ❏ Direct evidence of student learning and development, such as student products and performances resulting from embedded assignments, tests, and other educational experiences

- ❏ Indirect indicators such as surveys, placement, and other institutional research data. These indicators can provide both qualitative and quantitative information over time and across situations.

A more thorough discussion of course-embedded assessment techniques is presented in Chapter 3 of this handbook. It describes the relative uses of quantitative and qualitative information, as well as direct and indirect methods of evaluating student learning.

Examining Existing Practices for Success

Angelo, Ewell, and Lopez (2001) advocate building assessment plans and practices from those activities on campus that are already successful. When a "situation audit" of course-based, programmatic and/or institution-wide assessment is complete, local best practices will surface as models for additional assessment initiatives.

Faculty members and students probably already have a good sense of what is working best on a campus. For example, there may be anecdotal evidence that graduates of one program have particularly strong research skills, while students in another program may be especially adept at using and adapting what they have learned to solve unforeseen problems while working as interns. An audit of teaching and assessment practices used by successful programs will produce models for other departments.

Ideally, some of the faculty members or departments that have been evaluating student learning will have used the results of the evaluation to change practices and to enhance student learning. These efforts also can motivate and guide others in the institution.

The results of a comprehensive audit can serve as a baseline for forming a cohesive assessment plan (see Chapter 4). Data collected from the audit can be used to answer critical questions about which existing assessment practices on campus can form the core of the institution's assessment program and to identify the most critical gaps for which new assessment techniques are needed. Perhaps the most important benefit of conducting a situation audit is that the data gathered become a foundation for developing learning goals.

Starting with Successful Programs

Identifying successful programs and courses early can help later when organized assessment is started. Starting with the assessment of successful programs offers several benefits:

➤ **Effective teaching/learning efforts of faculty members and students are validated.**

➤ **The admissions, public relations, and development offices have substantive research information to use when publicizing the institution and its programs.**

➤ **External stakeholders have concrete, rather than anecdotal, evidence of the quality of the institution and its programs.**

➤ **Faculty members and administrators in other programs can learn from the successes of their colleagues.**

Defining Learning Goals before Selecting Assessment Methods

The most important step in developing successful methods for evaluating student learning is to develop meaningful, clear, and realistic goals for student learning at the course, program, or institutional level. These goals or statements of expected student learning are different from the actual evidence or the data gleaned from evaluations of student learning. Goals are the basis for determining how best to collect, assess, and interpret the data in order to improve. Data collection not tailored to goals will not provide information about the achievement of desired student learning, nor will it lead to new approaches to teaching and learning.

The goals or statements of student learning are hypotheses for what qualities or attributes will characterize students after they have completed a course or program, or after they have graduated from the college or the university.

The data generated from actual tests, surveys, or instruments used to gauge the outcome of the educational experience are the actual assessments[2].

For example, the learning goal might be to develop analytical skill. After a student has taken a course intended to promote this skill, he or she should have better analytical skill. This abstraction, analytical skill—the quality or attribute that students should possess after taking the course—is a generalized notion of what should be achieved. To evaluate the achievement of analytical skill, a test of learning might include problems that can be solved with syllogisms. The syllogistic problems "operationally define"—i.e., make concrete the abstraction "analytical skill." Thus, success in solving the problems (as indicated by scores above the norm, scores that surpass pretest scores, or scores that differ from those of similar students who did not take the same course) would indicate success in acquiring analytical skill.

Another way to move from the abstract to the specific when articulating student learning goals is to state those goals in terms of what, specifically, a student should be able to do in order to demonstrate that desired learning has occurred. In other words, what observable student behaviors should result from a learning experience? For example, astronomy faculty members may agree that their students will understand basic concepts about the solar system, but they may have differing opinions about what constitutes "basic concepts" and what it means to "understand" them. Do "basic concepts" refer to basic facts about each planet or also to theories about how the solar system was created? Should students memorize those basic facts, or should they be able to use information about our solar system to speculate about the characteristics of other solar systems?

It is important, therefore, to understand that the qualities or attributes that students should exhibit after a learning experience should be operationally

---

2 In research terms, educational experiences are the "independent variable or treatment," the assessments are the methods, and their results would be called the "dependent variable." The student learning outcomes, then, *depend* upon the educational experiences.

defined in order to be assessed meaningfully. For example, a statement of student learning (a learning goal) might be that a student will think critically after completing an introductory course in philosophy. Another learning goal might be that, after completing a service-learning course, a student have greater appreciation for others who are different. Each of these goals can be operationally defined, and then learning can be documented by a test or other instrument created to assess the specific goal. The results of the assessment demonstrate (or do not) the outcome one would expect to see—i.e., What would a student's performance on this particular assessment look like if he or she is a critical thinker? What would the student's performance look like if he or she is a person with appreciation for differences between people?

Appendix 6 is a worksheet for an exercise that faculty and staff members can use to begin to develop learning goals for courses and programs and to begin to think about how those goals might be achieved, how they might be assessed, and how a course or program might be altered to ensure greater student learning. The worksheet contains space for only three goals, in order to emphasize that the focus should be on important goals.

The remainder of this chapter 2 is devoted to developing learning goals; Chapter 3 is devoted to evaluating those goals.

Ensuring the Quality and Relevance of Learning Goal Statements

The institution can ensure the quality and relevance of learning goal statements by focusing on those that are most important, widely accepted by the various stakeholders, meaningful, sufficiently explicit, and interconnected among the various academic levels and curricula within the institution.

Key Learning Outcomes

Effective statements of expected student learning are focused on the most important goals of a course, program, or institution. They are not a collective list of goals that are idiosyncratic to a few faculty or staff members. Attempts to evaluate every possible goal can overwhelm an institution with tasks,

provide too much information, and dilute the focus on areas that need the most attention.

The departmental, school, or institutional mission statement, as described in *Characteristics* (Standard 1), should provide the basis for determining the most important goals at each level. It is useful to concentrate statements of expected learning outcomes by asking, "What are the *most* important learning outcomes we seek for our students in the context of the goals of our institution/program?" For example, the programs and learning outcomes of an institution whose mission includes giving each student a strong spiritual grounding may emphasize different learning outcomes from those of an institution whose mission includes teaching its students technical skills.

Widely Agreed-upon Concepts

Statements of expected learning outcomes will not be effective unless they are developed collaboratively and widely accepted by stakeholders: faculty members, students, employers, alumni, and others affected by or concerned with the program or institution. While it is unlikely that there will be unanimous agreement on expected learning outcomes, there should be a shared sense among most members regarding which learning is most important. The mission of the institution and the subsidiary missions of departments and programs serve as the natural sources for shared expectations.

Communication of Learning Goals

If the institutional community shares learning goals and if they are expressed clearly, then the resulting statements of expected learning outcomes can be used by the entire campus community. Clearly-expressed expectations for the learning outcomes of courses and programs can help students to focus their studies and, as a result, to learn more effectively. Prospective students who are aware of the specific types of expected learning outcomes of a program to which they are considering applying can make a better-informed decision about whether the program meets their needs, especially when evidence is available that those goals actually are achieved.

Faculty members who teach prerequisite courses or "service" courses can prepare students better for later courses and programs if they are familiar with the expected learning outcomes of subsequent courses or courses in the target program. For example, faculty members in the English department who are familiar with the expected learning outcomes of the theater department's programs and courses can better meet the needs of theater students taking literature courses, and physics faculty members can meet the needs of engineering students.

Meaningful Learning Goal Statements That Lead to Improvement

Meaningful statements of student learning goals address learning as a multidimensional and integrated process, occurring over time. They do not focus on trivial learning outcomes. Stated cogently and clearly, meaningful learning goals will lead to the improvement of teaching and learning at the course, program, and institutional levels. The importance of each learning goal should be obvious to students, faculty, and prospective employers.

Meaningful learning goals stress generalizable and higher-order thinking skills rather than memorization of facts or very simple conceptual understanding. For example, a goal to identify grammatical forms (past participles, etc.) is, in most cases, not as meaningful as a goal of being able to write and speak grammatically. Similarly, the successful memorization of important historical dates is not as meaningful as a goal for students to be able to place historical events within a social and political context, to draw meaningful comparisons between events, and to analyze current events within an historical framework. For both of these examples of more meaningful or higher-order goals, the more trivial goals of memorizing dates and acquiring the names of parts of speech probably will be achieved naturally in the course of achieving the larger goal.

Sufficiently Explicit Learning Goals

Although it is not helpful for statements of student learning goals to be so specific that they focus on unimportant or trivial outcomes, it is important for statements to be sufficiently *explicit* for all

stakeholders to have a common understanding of their meaning.

For instance, one goal for an undergraduate psychology program might be for students to exhibit proficiency in conducting research. While faculty members may implicitly understand what this goal might mean, increasing the specificity of the goal would enhance its clarity and allow for more direct assessment of the attainment of the goal. For example, a statement of the goal might read: "Students will learn the statistical, organizational, writing, and analytical skills necessary to conduct meaningful and valid scientific research." Statements then could describe the evidence needed to demonstrate that students have achieved the kowledge and abilities related to each of these components.

Interconnectedness of Student Learning Goals

Student learning can occur at many levels and in many venues:

❑ Course, program, and institutional levels (Standard 14);

❑ Undergraduate, graduate, and professional program levels (Standard 11);

❑ General education curricula (Standard 12);

❑ Related educational activities, such as basic skills, certificate programs, experiential learning, non-credit offerings, and distance or distributed learning (Standard 13); and

❑ In co-curricular and extracurricular activities (Standard 9).

An institution's curriculum may address particular learning outcomes in different complementary or overlapping courses and programs. Statements of learning outcomes for courses or programs should recognize and clarify these relationships, and student learning outcomes assessment plans should be structured to avoid duplication.

Choosing Learning Goals

Start with success

Determine which learning goals are already being assessed and what data may be available to assess other goals
  - ➤ Institutional Level
  - ➤ Program Level
  - ➤ Course Level

Ensure relevance of goals
  - ➤ Identify key learning outcomes
  - ➤ Use widely agreed-upon concepts
  - ➤ Communicate goals
  - ➤ Select important and meaningful goals
  - ➤ Be explicit
  - ➤ Integrate goals in different areas and levels

Choose goals that can lead to improvement

Emphasize higher-order thinking skills

Define learning goals before choosing assessment methods
  - ➤ Operationally define each goal
  - ➤ Tailor data collection to defined goals

Resources for Creating Student Learning Goal Statements

This section includes a discussion of several specific resources for crafting actual statements of student learning goals. Each of these resources presents opportunities both for "brainstorming" and for comprehensively and systematically reviewing sets of possible goals.

Existing Learning Goals

An institution already may have explicit and clear statements of student learning goals in place, and it is important to resist the urge to redesign entire sets of course, program, or institutional goals if they already exist. The focus should be on developing those that are missing, those that are unclear, those that have changed, or those that are complementary. For instance, many institutions developed learning goals for general education programs when those programs were initially created, and some may have been substantially revised during subsequent program review. However, faculty members may determine that no measures are being used to assess whether the goals have been achieved. The goals, then, may not need to be re-written; instead, they should be evaluated for their importance and relevance, and they should be supplemented with additional goals where appropriate. Of course, it is still important to measure student outcomes in these areas.

Existing Syllabi and Course Descriptions

Existing syllabi and catalogue descriptions provide a logical starting point for developing learning goals at the course level, because many faculty members already include learning goals in their syllabi, and many course descriptions include statements about course content, goals, and/or what the student should be able to do once the course is completed. Existing goals such as these can be reviewed for their relevance to programmatic mission, and faculty members should be encouraged to think about whether these goals reflect the current or changing focus of their disciplines. Examples of syllabi that already address learning goals can serve as resources for faculty members who have not previously developed goals, and faculty members familiar with the process can serve as mentors.

Leading Questions

Leading questions also can serve as the basis for a brainstorming exercise in developing learning goals.

The leading questions listed in Figure 3 can be tailored to apply to any discipline and can be refined to address more specific outcomes. In general, they focus attention on the most important learning goals for individual programs.

The following additional questions related to basic improvement are adapted from the work of Stufflebeam (2001):

❑ What alternative educational practices and experiences are available, and what are their comparative advantages over current practices at our institution?

❑ What are the characteristics of a good syllabus that can serve as a guide to teaching and learning?

❑ What facilities, materials, and equipment are needed to ensure success in reaching our educational objectives?

❑ What are the roles of faculty members, students, and others in the pursuit of learning?

❑ Is the course providing learning experiences for all of the students who are enrolled?

❑ Is a particular course worth the required institutional investment?

❑ Is the course meeting the minimum accreditation requirements for the discipline?

❑ Is the course equal to or better than analogous courses at comparable institutions?

Analysis of Student Work

The work products and performances of students that are the result of existing assignments and tests may already embody the important learning outcomes, even though the faculty member may not have explicitly conceived or stated those goals.

A retrospective review can suggest how the original statements of goals might be revised, especially if the unstated learning goals are important and if the evaluation methods are valid.

For instance, a political history course may not have the explicit goal of increasing awareness of and participation in current political events. Nevertheless, after taking the course, students may report increased civic awareness, an increased tendency to vote, and increased participation in local political activity. Therefore, it may make sense to make the development of political awareness an explicit course goal and to revise the course accordingly.

Inventory of Teaching Goals

Faculty members and students can use the Teaching Goals Inventory (Angelo and Cross, 1993), shown in Figure 4, to identify the priority of various learning goals in courses and programs. For example, individuals or groups of faculty members could use the inventory to understand better their expectations for a single course, a course with many sections, or a series of courses. They can use the inventory to review faculty documents, to examine existing disciplinary accreditation guidelines and standards, and to analyze direct evidence of student learning and development. Students also could complete the inventory so that the institution can determine whether students and faculty share the same perceptions about the relative priority of different types of learning.

Figure 3

Leading Questions for Developing Learning Goals

Questions for Faculty

- ❑ In general, what are the most important things a student gains from your field of study?
- ❑ What qualities and capabilities do you strive to foster in your students?
- ❑ What is the most important knowledge that your students acquire from your field of study or from working with you?
- ❑ How does your field of study or your work change the way students view themselves?
- ❑ In what ways does your field of study or what you do contribute to a student's well being?
- ❑ How does your field or what you do change the way a student looks at the world?
- ❑ What does your field of study or what you do contribute to the well being of society at large?
- ❑ How do people in this area of study differ from those in other areas (knowledge, skills, and/or values)?
- ❑ How do we know the extent to which students are learning what we hope from our field of study?
- ❑ How do we use information about student learning and development to enhance student learning?

Questions for Students

- ❑ What is the most important knowledge you have gained from taking courses, minoring, or majoring in this subject?
- ❑ What are the most valuable skills or abilities that have you developed as a result of taking courses, minoring, or majoring in this subject?
- ❑ How has taking courses, minoring, or majoring in this subject changed the way you look at yourself?
- ❑ How has taking courses, minoring, or majoring in this subject changed the way you look at the world?
- ❑ How has taking courses, minoring, or majoring in this subject changed the way you think about the future?
- ❑ How do you know whether these changes have occurred?
- ❑ How do people in this area of study differ from those in other areas (knowledge, skills, and/or values)?
- ❑ What changes might be made in course and programs of your major or minor to enhance student learning?

Based on leading questions developed by Prof. C. Ewart, Department of Psychology, Syracuse University, 1998. Reproduced with permission.

Figure 4

Teaching Goals Inventory
Self-Scorable Version

Purpose

The *Teaching Goals Inventory* (TGI) is a self-assessment of instructional goals.

Its purpose is three-fold: (1) To help college teachers become more aware of what they want to accomplish in individual courses; (2) To help faculty locate Classroom Assessment Techniques they can adapt and use to assess how well they are achieving their teaching and learning goals; and, (3) To provide a starting point for discussions of teaching and learning goals among colleagues.

Directions

Please select ONE course you are currently teaching. Respond to each item on the Inventory in relation to that particular course. (Your responses might be quite different if you were asked about your *overall* teaching and learning goals, for example, or the appropriate instructional goals for your discipline.)

Just to remind yourself, please print the title of the specific course you are focusing on below:

_____

Please rate the importance of each of the 52 goals listed below to the specific course you have selected. Assess each goal in terms of what you deliberately aim to have your students accomplish, rather than in terms of the goal's general worthiness or overall importance to your institution's mission. There are no "right" or "wrong" answers; only personally accurate or inaccurate ones.

For each goal, circle *only one* response on the 1 to 5 rating scale. You may find it helpful to quickly read through all 52 goals *before* rating their relative importance.

In relation to the course you are focusing on, indicate whether each goal rated is:

(5) **Essential**	A goal you ***always/nearly always*** try to achieve (76% to 100% of the time)
(4) **Very Important**	A goal you ***very often*** try to achieve (51% to 75% of the time)
(3) **Important**	A goal you ***sometimes*** try to achieve (26% to 50% of the time)
(2) **Unimportant**	A goal you ***rarely*** try to achieve (1% to 25% of the time) or
(1) **Not Applicable**	A goal you ***never*** try to achieve.

Please note: This Inventory was developed with support from The Pew Charitable Trusts and the Ford Foundation by K. P. Cross & T. A. Angelo, U. C. Berkeley School of Education, 1992. Reproduced with permission of the authors.

Rate the importance of each goal below in terms of what you aim to have students accomplish in your course.	Essential	Very Important	Important	Unimportant	Not Applicable
1. Develop ability to apply principles and generalizations already learned to new problems and situations	5	4	3	2	1
2. Develop analytic skills	5	4	3	2	1
3. Develop problem-solving skills	5	4	3	2	1
4. Develop ability to draw reasonable inferences from observations	5	4	3	2	1
5. Develop ability to synthesize and integrate information and ideas	5	4	3	2	1
6. Develop ability to think holistically: to see the whole as well as the parts	5	4	3	2	1
7. Develop ability to think creatively	5	4	3	2	1
8. Develop ability to distinguish between fact and opinion	5	4	3	2	1
9. Improve skill at paying attention	5	4	3	2	1
10. Develop ability to concentrate	5	4	3	2	1
11. Improve memory skills	5	4	3	2	1
12. Improve listening skills	5	4	3	2	1
13. Improve speaking skills	5	4	3	2	1
14. Improve reading skills	5	4	3	2	1
15. Improve writing skills	5	4	3	2	1
16. Develop appropriate study skills, strategies, and habits	5	4	3	2	1
17. Improve mathematical skills	5	4	3	2	1
18. Learn terms and facts of this subject	5	4	3	2	1
19. Learn concepts and theories in this subject	5	4	3	2	1
20. Develop skill in using materials, tools, and/or technology central to this subject	5	4	3	2	1
21. Learn to understand perspectives and values of this subject	5	4	3	2	1
22. Prepare for transfer or graduate study	5	4	3	2	1

K. P. Cross & T. A. Angelo, U.C. Berkeley School of Education, 1992

Rate the importance of each goal below in terms of what you aim to have students accomplish in your course.	Essential	Very Important	Important	Unimportant	Not Applicable
23. Learn techniques and methods used to gain new knowledge in this subject	5	4	3	2	1
24. Learn to evaluate methods and materials in this subject	5	4	3	2	1
25. Learn to appreciate important contributions to this subject	5	4	3	2	1
26. Develop an appreciation of the liberal arts and sciences	5	4	3	2	1
27. Develop an openness to new ideas	5	4	3	2	1
28. Develop an informed concern about contemporary social issues	5	4	3	2	1
29. Develop a commitment to exercise the rights and responsibilities of citizenship	5	4	3	2	1
30. Develop a lifelong love of learning	5	4	3	2	1
31. Develop aesthetic appreciations	5	4	3	2	1
32. Develop an informed historical perspective	5	4	3	2	1
33. Develop an informed understanding of the role of science and technology	5	4	3	2	1
34. Develop an informed appreciation of other cultures	5	4	3	2	1
35. Develop capacity to make informed ethical choices	5	4	3	2	1
36. Develop ability to work productively with others	5	4	3	2	1
37. Develop management skills	5	4	3	2	1
38. Develop leadership skills	5	4	3	2	1
39. Develop a commitment to accurate work	5	4	3	2	1
40. Improve ability to follow directions, instructions, and plans	5	4	3	2	1
41. Improve ability to organize and use time effectively	5	4	3	2	1
42. Develop a commitment to personal achievement	5	4	3	2	1
43. Develop ability to perform skillfully	5	4	3	2	1

K. P. Cross & T. A. Angelo, U.C. Berkeley School of Education, 1992

Rate the importance of each goal below in terms of what you aim to have students accomplish in your course.	Essential	Very Important	Important	Unimportant	Not Applicable
44. Cultivate a sense of responsibility for one's own behavior	5	4	3	2	1
45. Improve self-esteem/self-confidence	5	4	3	2	1
46. Develop a commitment to one's own values	5	4	3	2	1
47. Develop respect for others	5	4	3	2	1
48. Cultivate emotional health and well-being	5	4	3	2	1
49. Cultivate physical health and well-being	5	4	3	2	1
50. Cultivate an active commitment to honesty	5	4	3	2	1
51. Develop capacity to think for one's self	5	4	3	2	1
52. Develop capacity to make wise decisions	5	4	3	2	1

Self-Scoring Worksheet

1. In all, how many of the 52 goals did you rate as "Essential"? ____

2. How many "Essential" goals did you identify in each of the six clusters listed below?

Cluster Number and Name	Goals included in cluster	Total number of "Essential" goals in each cluster	Clusters Ranked (1st to 6th) by number of "Essential" goals included
I. Higher-Order Thinking Skills	1 - 8	_____	_____
II. Basic Academic Success Skills	9 - 17	_____	_____
III. Discipline-Specific Knowledge & Skills	18-25	_____	_____
IV. Liberal Arts & Academic Values	26-35	_____	_____
V. Work and Career Preparation	36-43	_____	_____
VI. Personal Development	44-52	_____	_____

K. P. Cross & T. A. Angelo, U.C. Berkeley School of Education, 1992

3

Evaluating Student Learning

There are many ways to approach the evaluation of student learning. The characteristics of good evidence of student learning include considerations of direct and indirect methods for gathering evidence of student learning, the appropriate use of quantitative and qualitative evidence, and other methodological considerations. First, however, it is important to understand the fundamental assessment concepts of formative and summative assessment and benchmarking.

Formative and Summative Assessment

Formative assessment is ongoing assessment that is intended to improve an individual student's performance, student learning outcomes at the course or program level, or overall institutional effectiveness. By its nature, formative assessment is used internally, primarily by those responsible for teaching a course or developing a program.

Ideally, formative assessment allows a professor, professional staff member, or program director to act quickly to adjust the contents or approach of a course or program. For instance, a faculty member might revise his or her next unit after reviewing students' performance on an examination at the end of the first unit, rather than simply forging ahead with the pre-designated contents of the course. Many instructors also solicit repeated brief evaluations of their teaching, and the data gleaned from these can be used to make adjustments that may improve learning, such as the introduction of more discussion into a class.

In contrast, summative assessment occurs at the end of a unit, course, or program. The purposes of this type of assessment are to determine whether or not overall goals have been achieved and to provide information on performance for an individual student or statistics about a course or program for internal or external accountability purposes. Grades are the most common form of summative assessment.

Goals for student learning will be expressed summatively when faculty members are describing what they expect students to be able to do or what skills they expect students to achieve when they complete a course or a program or when they graduate from the institution.

Formative and summative assessment work together to improve learning. They should be central components of assessment at the course level, and where appropriate, at the program level.

Benchmarking

The term benchmarking is now common in assessment plans and conversations about assessment. Originally, benchmarking was a term used in the corporate environment to define a set of external standards against which an organization could measure itself. The organization identifies comparable, peer, or "reach" organizations and systematically compares its practices or achievements against those of the other organization.

In higher education settings, a university might use benchmarking techniques to define its comparison group—its peer institutions—and to compare its own outcomes to theirs. This benchmarking could be based, for example, on retention rates, five-year graduation rates, admissions yield data (the number of enrollees as a function of the number of students accepted), employment and graduate school placement rates, and performance on national or professional examinations. Theoretically, any outcome for which there are data from peer institutions and programs can be compared in a benchmarking study.

Two other related forms of benchmarking are used in higher education settings. A college or university can compare itself to a national norm by reviewing the data from a published test or survey such as the National Survey of Student Engagement (NSSE). Alternatively or in addition, an institution can set for itself the goals or benchmarks that it hopes to achieve within a specified time period (e.g., to increase job placement rates from 70% to 90% in five years).

The benefit of inter-institutional comparison is that it can flag problem areas to investigate the causes of results that differ from the norm. For example, two comparable liberal arts colleges with similar selectivity, similar student preparedness, similar socioeconomic profiles for their students, and similar science curricula, may discover that proportionately more students are accepted to medical schools from one institution than from another. Further investigation may reveal that the excelling college requires a hospital internship for all of its pre-med students.

The discovery that an institution's students are below the norm on a national metric (e.g., amount of time devoted to school work outside the classroom) challenges the institution to determine the reason for this result. Similarly, an institution that sets its own internal benchmarks must design and implement a program to achieve its goals.

Before beginning to articulate goals for student learning, program faculty and leaders of institutional assessment should consider how the use of benchmarks could enhance their institution's ability to achieve its goals and whether useful measures from comparable peer institutions are available.

Direct and Indirect Methods for Assessing Student Learning

The concepts of direct and indirect methods of evaluating student learning are often confused with each other and with quantitative and qualitative forms of information. Each of these has its merits and drawbacks.

Direct and indirect methods of evaluating learning relate to whether or not the method provides evidence in the form of student products or performances. Such evidence demonstrates that *actual learning* has occurred relating to a specific content or skill. Indirect methods reveal characteristics associated with learning, but they only imply that learning has occurred. These characteristics may relate to the student, such as perceptions of student learning, or they may relate to the institution, such as graduation rates.

When a student completes a calculus problem correctly and shows her work, learning is demonstrated *directly*. When the same student describes her own calculus abilities as excellent, she is demonstrating *indirectly* that she has learned calculus. Both of these pieces of information about the student's performance are important. For excample, a student's perception that she is doing poorly in calculus when she is actually doing well would provide important information to both the student and the professor. However, indirect evidence—in this case, a perception—is less meaningful without the associated direct and tangible evidence of learning.

Figure 5 includes examples of direct and indirect measures of student learning at the course, program, and institutional levels. Many of the examples presented in Figure 5 can be used as measures of student learning at more than one level. For example, portfolios of student work and student satisfaction surveys can be used at the course, program, and institutional level, and internship performance ratings could be used at the course or program level.

Figure 5

Examples of Direct and Indirect Measures of Student Learning (Course, Program, and Institutional Levels)

	Direct Measures	**Indirect Measures**
Course	❈ Course and homework assignments ❈ Examinations and quizzes ❈ Standardized tests ❈ Term papers and reports ❈ Observations of field work, internship performance, service learning, or clinical experiences ❈ Research projects ❈ Class discussion participation ❈ Case study analysis ❈ Rubric (a criterion-based rating scale) scores for writing, oral presentations, and performances ❈ Artistic performances and products ❈ Grades that are based on explicit criteria related to clear learning goals	❈ Course evaluations ❈ Test blueprints (outlines of the concepts and skills covered on tests) ❈ Percent of class time spent in active learning ❈ Number of student hours spent on service learning ❈ Number of student hours spent on homework ❈ Number of student hours spent at intellectual or cultural activities related to the course ❈ Grades that are not based on explicit criteria related to clear learning goals
Program	❈ Capstone projects, senior theses, exhibits, or performances ❈ Pass rates or scores on licensure, certification, or subject area tests ❈ Student publications or conference presentations ❈ Employer and internship supervisor ratings of students' performance	❈ Focus group interviews with students, faculty members, or employers ❈ Registration or course enrollment information ❈ Department or program review data ❈ Job placement ❈ Employer or alumni surveys ❈ Student perception surveys ❈ Proportion of upper-level courses compared to the same program at other institutions ❈ Graduate school placement rates
Institutional	❈ Performance on tests of writing, critical thinking, or general knowledge ❈ Rubric (criterion-based rating scale) scores for class assignments in General Education, interdisciplinary core courses, or other courses required of all students ❈ Performance on achievement tests ❈ Explicit self-reflections on what students have learned related to institutional programs such as service learning (e.g., asking students to name the three most important things they have learned in a program).	❈ Locally-developed, commercial, or national surveys of student perceptions or self-report of activities (e.g., National Survey of Student Engagement) ❈ Transcript studies that examine patterns and trends of course selection and grading ❈ Annual reports including institutional benchmarks, such as graduation and retention rates, grade point averages of graduates, etc.

Direct Methods

Direct methods of evaluating student learning are those that provide evidence of whether or not a student has command of a specific subject or content area, can perform a certain task, exhibits a particular skill, demonstrates a certain quality in his or her work (e.g., creativity, analysis, synthesis, or objectivity), or holds a particular value. Direct methods can be used at the course level, the program level, and, theoretically, at the institutional level.

Course Level. Most familiar are direct evaluations of learning that are applied at the course level. Examinations,[3] regardless of format, are designed to be direct evaluations of student learning. Similarly, evaluations of writing samples, presentations, artistic performances, and exhibits provide direct evidence of student learning, as do evaluations of student performance in internships, research projects, field work, or service learning settings. As discussed later, grading linked to clear learning goals is a valid and useful form of direct measurement of student learning.

Program Level. At the program level, examinations also are used frequently as direct measures of student learning. Such examinations would be more comprehensive than those embedded within a course and would be designed to evaluate cumulative, aggregate, or holistic learning after the conclusion of a program or during the course of the program.

For example, a writing examination might be given after the first two years of a general education program, with the goal of determining whether students' writing was enhanced as a function of the program. Standardized tests of disciplinary content might be administered to students after they have completed all program requirements for the major (e.g., American Chemical Society examinations). Honors theses, senior theses, or senior projects are other sources of direct evidence of student learning within a program. Ratings by internship supervisors of how well interns are demonstrating key learning outcomes are important, direct program-level evidence of student learning.

Institutional Level. Direct evaluations at the institutional level are used less frequently and are much more likely to take the form of an examination. A college or university might use the Academic Profile or the Major Field Tests from the Educational Testing Service, the Collegiate Assessment of Academic Proficiency from the ACT (American College Testing) or other graduate-level examination scores to demonstrate that learning has occurred.

An institution may wish to demonstrate that certain goals expressed in its mission were achieved through exposure to the entirety of its curriculum and co-curricular experiences. For example, it may wish to show that regardless of program or major, which co-curricular activities students have participated in, and whether students were residents or commuters, they exhibit cultural sensitivity and global cultural and geographical awareness. It could design an evaluation process to determine the degree to which graduating students exhibited these qualities (e.g., a rubric for reviewing an examination or portfolio).

It may appear that such qualities are abstract and, therefore, that the measurement of learning was not direct, but in fact that is not the case. In this example, the goal was to have students learn, through curricular and co-curricular programs, to be good global citizens, broadly speaking, and the hypothetical examination was designed to measure the degree to which this goal was achieved.

General education knowledge, competencies, and skills gained across the curriculum might be evaluated over the entire student experience, whether before or after graduation.

---

3 For the purpose of clarity, the term "examination" is being used here to refer to what are commonly called quizzes, exams, or tests designed to measure whether or not a student has learned something that he or she was taught prior to its administration. The word "test" is a more generic term and can apply to any measure that may be direct or indirect, or qualitative or quantitative.

Fundamental Importance of Direct Forms of Evaluation. The power of direct assessments of student learning is that, if designed properly, they answer the most important questions:

❏ What did students learn as a result of an educational experience?

❏ To what degree did students learn?

❏ What did students *not* learn?

Institutional stakeholders and the public can understand easily data gleaned from direct evaluations of student learning. They can understand, for instance, that students at Institution A have higher scores on the American Chemical Society examination than students at Institution B, and those same data provide assurance that a certain level of knowledge has been acquired by students at both institutions.

Limitations and Considerations Related to Direct Forms of Evaluation. Direct assessments, however, do not tell the whole story of student learning. There are two potential problems with using only direct assessments of student learning. The first problem relates only to direct methods, and the second pertains to both direct and indirect methods.

Direct assessments of student learning, while providing evidence of *what* the student has learned, provide no evidence as to why the student has learned or *why* he or she has not learned. The "why" of student learning is especially important when students have not learned, because one of the primary goals of assessment is to make future learning experiences more effective.

If students perform poorly on a mathematics exam, for instance, it is important for the instructor to know whether the students' performance resulted from not having learned the material or from having learned the material but also experiencing anxiety during the examination. Other data are needed to answer this question.

It is important to consider that even direct forms of evaluation do not necessarily indicate whether "value-added" learning has occurred. The Commission does not require that its member institutions demonstrate value-added learning, only

that the institution's learning outcomes are consistent with its goals.

In and of themselves, direct forms of evaluation do not always provide evidence that the targeted learning goal was achieved within the context of a course, a program, or an entire college education, or whether the demonstration of the learning goal was influenced by or a product of prior learning or even the result of innate abilities. If an institution or faculty members in a program are concerned about demonstrating that the learning occurred in a particular context, then care should be taken to design aspects of the assessment program to tap "value-added" learning.

At the course level, the contrast between value-added demonstrations of student learning and absolute levels of student learning is rarely meaningful. One can assume, for instance, that knowledge of college-level organic chemistry, elementary school teaching techniques, or Spinoza's philosophy was acquired within the context of the course specifically designed to teach that knowledge. The same reasoning applies to the program level; students are likely to have acquired the skills and knowledge specific to their programs while taking courses within the program.

At the institutional level, the distinction between student knowledge that was acquired before the student arrived at the institution and what he or she learned while in attending the institution may be a more salient one. Some institutions may want to demonstrate that the education they provide has had a fundamental effect on students' lives—i.e., changed them in a way that would not have occurred if the student did not attend college or attended a different type of college.

One college, for instance, may want to demonstrate that a personal atmosphere that encourages faculty-student mentoring relationships results in better preparation for acceptance to graduate school than a student might otherwise receive at a different type of institution. Another may want to demonstrate that it prepares its students for the real world in a way that a different college experience cannot. Yet another might use assessment data to show that students have dramatically increased their job marketability or their chances of graduating by attending the college.

If institutions seek to demonstrate such accomplishments, it is important to consider whether the assessment design truly demonstrates value-added learning rather than some other phenomenon. For instance, students entering an institution with very high SAT writing scores are likely to write well after they have been exposed to the college's General Education program. In other words, to the extent that high scores of graduating students on tests of writing skills reflect pre-college expertise, those scores reflect the effect(s) of one or more "inputs" but are not necessarily value-added.

Value-added gains can be useful in assuring the college community and the public that higher education provides cognitive, affective, and social growth beyond the levels the students had attained when they entered college. However, devoting too much attention to creating an assessment design that rules out other causes for student learning can take the focus away from the most important question: Have students who graduate from this college or university learned what the institution hoped they would learn?

Indirect Methods

Indirect methods of evaluating student learning involve data that are *related to* the act of learning, such as factors that predict or mediate learning or perceptions about learning but do not reflect learning itself. Indirect evidence often is acquired through the use of self-report format surveys, questionnaires, and interviews. Indirect evidence also is provided in the form of "demographic" statistics about the student population of an institution, such as overall GPA, student retention rates, graduation rates, and job placement rates. Qualitative information about graduates, such as names of employers, graduate schools attended, and alumni achievements are also common forms of indirect evidence.

Course Level. The most familiar indirect assessment of student learning is the course and/or teaching evaluation given at the end of the semester. These instruments usually have a quantitative section in a Likert (numerically-scaled) format, in which the student rates the quality of teaching and of the course, as well as a narrative section in which the student offers additional qualitative comments.

An instructor who regularly reviews his or her teaching evaluations and who changes the course as a result of those evaluations is engaging in improvement based on hypotheses derived from the indirect assessment of student learning. The same instructor can use this indirect method in conjunction with direct methods to improve student learning in the course.

For example, students might use the narrative portion of the evaluation to request more time for class discussion and might give the professor only moderate ratings for "engagement with the course material." The instructor decides to introduce more discussion into his or her class and subsequently students praise the use of discussion and give high ratings for the instructor's "engagement with course material." Most importantly, the instructor notices that student grades on quizzes or exams and work on assignments are higher in the semester after he made the change. This simple illustration of how indirect evidence can be used in conjunction with direct evidence can be applied in more complicated situations.

Program Level. At the program level, student satisfaction surveys may reveal that students want more one-on-one contact with faculty members. Upon reflection, faculty members may decide to offer more independent study experiences; consequently, scores on Graduate Record Examination subject area exams improve (direct evidence of student learning), as do graduate school admission rates (indirect evidence of student learning).

Institutional Level. Indirect means of evaluating student learning are important at the institutional level as well. National surveys, such as the National Survey of Student Engagement (NSSE), provide benchmarking opportunities for the institutions to gauge the qualities of their student populations relative to other institutions so that they can determine whether changes in programming affect students' perceptions and behavior inside and outside the classroom. Ultimately, such assessments can affect performance in the classroom.

For instance, if an institution finds that its students spend less time studying than the national average for study time, it might introduce curricular changes that link student evaluation (i.e., grades) more directly to the amount of time studied, perhaps by providing assignments that demand more out-of-class time and by using class examinations which test areas that are not learned simply by attending class. The greater engagement that these changes create might serve to improve student performance on direct measures of student learning.

Indirect evidence often focuses on the learning *process* and the learning *environment.* Alexander Astin's input-environment-output assessment model, based on research from the past several decades (e.g., Astin, 1991; Chickering & Gamson, 1991; Pascarella & Terenzini, 1991) indicates that students learn most effectively when, in general, they are engaged in the learning process and they can see a connection among course goals, course content, and evaluation.[4]

The extent to which these inputs and processes exist may support the inference that student learning is taking place. Each of these discoveries about student learning was gained through indirect methods of assessment, such as surveys of student perceptions and opinions. The results of these surveys then were correlated with actual student learning outcomes (measured directly), demonstrating that when the existence of specified inputs and processes correlates with student learning.

Limitations and Considerations Related to Indirect Methods of Evaluation. The most important limitation of indirect methods is that they do not evaluate student learning *per se,* and therefore should not be the only means of assessing outcomes.

As with direct measures of student learning, it is important to consider that indirect measures do not necessarily imply that value-added learning has occurred. Students who express indifference to co-curricular activities after their first year may be expressing an indifference that is the result of dissatisfaction with campus programs, or they may have arrived on campus disinclined to spend time on anything but course-related work.

As noted above, the Commission does not require proof of value-added student learning. Nevertheless, an institution should consider whether value-added data are necessary to demonstrate that it fulfills its own mission. If so, it should ensure that data collection procedures warrant conclusions about the effectiveness of programs in teaching students.

Quantitative vs. Qualitative Evidence

In every example of direct and indirect assessment cited above, the evaluation of student learning could provide either qualitative or quantitative information. Both qualitative and quantitative information are valuable forms of evidence about student outcomes.

Quantitative evidence consists of data that are represented numerically. For instance, performance on a test or responses to a questionnaire may be scored so that a number represents the degree to which an individual performed or agreed/disagreed with a certain concept. Because quantitative data are expressed in numbers, they can be compared directly or subjected to statistical analysis, and they can enable the researcher to make certain assumptions when comparing one data point to another. Quantitative data also may permit one to express numerically meaningful changes in performance (given certain conditions). One may claim, for instance, that a change in a test score from 50 to 60 represents a 10-point or a 20 percent gain in an individual's performance, expressed as a percentage of his or her original score. Quantitative data, therefore, are valued for the ease with which calculations and comparisons can be made, and for the easily understandable representations of performance that they produce.

Qualitative evidence typically comes in two forms. The first form involves simple categorization of individuals into discrete groups (e.g., employed or unemployed; participates in athletics or does not participate in athletics). The second form of qualitative evidence is data expressed in prose or narrative. A question is asked of an individual and

---

4 See Chapter 5 for a further discussion of this topic. See also Figure 21 for a list of conditions under which students learn most effectively.

he or she responds in a free-form manner, expressing, for instance, an idea, opinion, or evaluation. Because of their non-numerical nature, qualitative data cannot be subjected directly to statistical analyses, nor can easy direct comparisons be made without engaging in an intervening process to categorize or interpret the data. Qualitative data, however, can be "richer" than quantitative data, because they provide a more extensive variety of information related to a particular learning goal. Many faculty members, for instance, use the numerical scores (quantitative data) from their teaching evaluations to make overall judgments of their own performance, but they value the qualitative, narrative comments from students as more useful in revealing students' personal perceptions of a course.

A common misconception is that qualitative assessments are not as reliable, valid, or objective as quantitative ones. This is not necessarily the case. There are well-designed and statistically reliable means of interpreting and analyzing qualitative data and numerous resources for learning to use qualitative methods (see Silverman, 2001; Maxwell, 1996). For example, an instructor might assess the same learning goals using a multiple-choice test or an essay test. Similarly, an instructor might grade a senior project presentation quantitatively with a standard set of evaluation criteria (i.e., a rubric). Alternatively, he or she might provide the student with a prose evaluation, in a non-scaled format, citing the strengths and weaknesses of the presentation. However, it is best if this evaluation is organized around a standard set of criteria that were shared with the student beforehand.

A student survey designed to gather information on student satisfaction may elicit data that are quantitative (i.e., "On a scale of 1 to 7, how satisfied are you with the quality of advising?") or qualitative ("How would you describe your experience with academic advising?"). Similarly, employers asked to assess the strengths and weaknesses of alumni may be asked to assign "scores" to, or to describe, alumni characteristics.

Most beginning assessment initiatives are likely to rely more heavily on quantitative, rather than qualitative, forms of assessment for several reasons. Quantitative data are easier to collect and are in the form of a readily-analyzable numeric score. In contrast, qualitative data must be sorted, categorized, and interpreted (most often by humans rather than by computer programs) before a final judgment can occur. Methods of ensuring the reliability of qualitative data are time-consuming. For instance, to ensure that portfolio assessment is reliable, at least two raters are used to review each portfolio, providing a form of "inter-rater" reliability. Focus groups, another commonly used form of qualitative data collection, require large investments of time to gather data from comparatively few students.

A good use of qualitative evaluation is to help develop quantitative evaluation criteria (rubrics). For instance, one might conduct focus groups for the purpose of designing questions for a satisfaction questionnaire or use a scoring rubric for portfolios to determine what characteristics of students' writing might be evaluated.

For assessing student learning, *Characteristics* encourages the use of multiple approaches—both quantitative and qualitative—but it does not *require* the use of both approaches (see Standard 14). Institutions and faculty members in different programs should be thoughtful about which approach, or combination of approaches, best suits the student outcomes that are being assessed in each unique situation.

Other Methodological Considerations

Some of the other methodological considerations often raised with regard to assessment include reliability and validity; pretests, posttests, and longitudinal design; the role of grades, self-report measures, and statistical versus practical significance.

Validity and Reliability

In general, the terms "validity" and "reliability" refer to the extent to which assessment tools and methods provide accurate, fair, and useful information. Both concepts are important factors in choosing standardized assessment instruments and should be considered seriously when developing locally-created instruments for summative assessment.

Validity refers to the integrity of the instrument. Does the instrument measure what it was designed to measure, or does it actually measure something else? An instrument designed to assess student sensitivity to the cultural norms of others, for instance, may actually be measuring a student's sensitivity to detecting those responses desired by the professor or the institution that values such sensitivity. Obviously, the instrument would not provide a valid assessment of cultural sensitivity.

Three forms of validity are especially relevant to assessing student outcomes. An instrument with "construct validity" adequately taps the "construct" or conceptual framework that it is designed to measure because its questions have been developed specifically for that purpose. The test of cultural sensitivity described above lacks construct validity because it assesses student perceptions of faculty beliefs, not cultural sensitivity.

Content validity, and in particular "face validity," refers to the content and structure of an evaluation instrument: On the face of it, does it appear to assess what it is designed to assess (Gall, Borg & Gall, 1998). The cultural sensitivity instrument described above may appear to have face validity—the questions appear to be about cultural sensitivity—even though it lacks construct validity. In general, however, the content and structure of an instrument should make sense to those who are using it. Several methods are employed by test designers to ensure that instruments have both content and face validity.

A third important form of validity is referred to as "concurrent" or "criterion validity." Criterion validity means that a test or assessment instrument will yield results that are similar to those of other instruments designed to assess the same outcome. Two tests of college mathematics ability, for instance, should yield similar results when administered to the same students; if one measure of student satisfaction demonstrates that students are very satisfied, another should as well. This result also could demonstrate "predictive validity" if the strength of the correlation between the two measures was great. A test or other evaluation instrument with good criterion validity also will predict performance on other measures of constructs that should be related. For instance, student satisfaction should predict retention, and

high scores on a test of ethical decision-making should predict ethical behavior. Additional concepts and examples related to reliability and validity are discussed in the section below entitled, "Key questions for choosing assessment instruments."

Reliability refers to the consistency of results for a test or assessment instrument over repeated administrations to the same individuals. For instance, an aptitude test for mechanical engineering, given twice to the same person, should yield similar results each time. Otherwise, it fails in its purpose of providing an accurate prediction of future success in mechanical engineering.

Reliability is established during the development of the test, when special populations are recruited to take the test more than once, before the test is used for its intended purpose. Reliability information about standardized tests is presented in the form of statistical correlations (which should be very high) among repeated administrations of the test in the same population.

The concepts of validity and reliability apply primarily to summative assessment, and not as directly to formative assessment, because instructor-created examinations and measures usually only exhibit "face validity," not the other forms of validity discussed here, and they are not usually subjected to rigorous pre-administration tests of reliability.

Pretests, Posttests, and Longitudinal Designs

A common misconception is that, in order to make any claims about "value-added" changes in student learning, one must use a pretest-posttest format. For instance, in order to demonstrate that a general education program has improved the writing skills of students, it appears that it would be necessary to have data on the writing skills of the *same* students before they began the program. This notion could thwart attempts to assess writing skills, and in a large institutional setting, it could be so daunting that it could short-circuit any attempt to demonstrate that writing skills have improved.

Two conceptual alternatives to a pretest-posttest are discussed briefly below. Research methods experts on most campuses could further explain these and suggest additional alternatives.

The first option would be to identify which general education experiences were designed specifically to enhance writing skill. Perhaps these experiences include courses in introductory composition, rhetoric, and an initial writing-intensive course in the major. One then could compare two populations of first-year students or two populations of sophomores—those who had completed these courses with those who had not. The group that has not completed the courses can serve as the comparison or "control" against the group that competed the courses.

A second option is to compare students against a national norm on a standardized test or against a targeted "benchmark" population. Suppose the learning goal in question is that students have gained a certain level of mathematical proficiency as a consequence of taking a two-course mathematics sequence in a general education program. One can administer a standardized test of college-level mathematics after students have completed the sequence and compare students' scores to national norms. In this case, no pretest was necessary; the national norm serves as the comparison or "control" group. This method is problematic if students at the institution are not drawn from an average population, as would be the case if the institution is highly selective or open-access. However, it does produce meaningful comparisons if an institution's student population roughly approximates an average population. Scholastic Achievement Test scores, for instance, might be used as a measure of the level of selectiveness used in admitting students.

If the institution's population is not average, a benchmarking strategy would be a more appropriate alternative. Students' scores on a test of college mathematics could be compared to the scores of students at institutions with comparable populations. Scores higher than those of the benchmarked school would be convincing evidence that the math curriculum of the target institution is successful.

A common assertion is that longitudinal research designs (those that follow the same individuals over time) are necessary to draw meaningful conclusions about what students have learned. Sometimes a longitudinal perspective is warranted because other approaches are less valid. For example, if an

institution is interested in demonstrating that its graduates are successful in their careers, a longitudinal survey administered to graduates repeatedly over several years would be appropriate for several reasons. Demographic data tell us, for instance, that people change careers multiple times during their lives, so examination of a single "window" of time may not be an accurate assessment. In addition, the population of graduates offers the benefit that its members will be around long enough to be surveyed repeatedly over time.

Most importantly, however, a longitudinal design guards against "cohort effects" that could intrude if graduates from one generation were compared with graduates from another generation. Career trajectories may change historically, and the character of the institution may have been markedly different in the past. Thus, 1950s female graduates may hold a lower percentage of professional degrees than 1980s female graduates. This finding tells us more about historical context than institutional outcomes. However, the same question, asked of the same individuals at several different points in time yields meaningful information. A finding that female students from the same cohort had a greater percentage of graduate degrees 20 years after college than they did 10 years after college could be used (in conjunction with other outcomes data) to demonstrate that the institution produces lifelong learners.

In most cases, when student outcomes during or at the end of a higher education experience are being evaluated, longitudinal data are not necessary and may not yield meaningful information. Pre-test and post-test assessments, as well as alternatives which are discussed above, are more practical alternatives and provide answers to the same general question: "Has meaningful learning occurred as a result of an educational experience?"

Where Do Grades Fit into the Picture?

Faculty members and others often ask whether grades are appropriate and sufficient for assessment of student learning after the learning goals are defined. The answer is that grades have been, and will continue to be, an excellent indicator of student learning *if they are appropriately linked to learning goals*. The Commission recognizes that grades are an effective measure of student achievement if there is a demonstrable relationship between the goals and objectives for student learning and the particular bases (such as assignments and examinations) upon which student achievement is evaluated (Standard 14).

In and of themselves, however, grades are not direct evidence of student learning. That is, a numeric or a letter grade alone does not express the *content* of what students have learned; it reflects only the degree to which the student is perceived to have learned in a specific context.

One reason "grade inflation" is seen as a problem is that grades alone cannot be relied on to reflect student performance accurately. One could ask: "Does one grade of 'A' equal another?" If instructors were to match grades explicitly with goals, it would become easier to combat grade inflation, because high grades must reflect high performance in specified areas.

Grades, however, can provide an excellent means for improving teaching and learning both during a course (formatively) and at the conclusion of a course (summatively). When grades serve as the final judgment of performance in a course, they provide a summative evaluation of students' performance as individuals and as a class. If the grades of individual students can be traced directly to their respective competencies in a course, the learning achievements of those students are being assessed in a meaningful fashion. If, however, examinations or homework assignments are not designed to test the skills and competencies that the course was designed to teach, then grades for that course are measuring something other than student attainment of the course goals.

Suppose, for instance, an instructor presents the content of an anatomy and physiology course that focuses on identifying and labeling anatomical structures and physiological processes. An appropriate evaluation of student mastery of the course content would be an objective final exam requiring students to label diagrams, answer multiple-choice definitional questions, and fill in the blanks. In contrast, an examination that required students to evaluate a physiology experiment on its methodological merits would not be an assessment of student learning of the course content. Some

students would do well on the essay exam, but their performance probably would not be related to what they learned in the course. In this example, a bad grade could not be attributed to a student's failure to learn the material or to prepare for the examination. Thus, even the use of grades as a summative assessment warrants a careful approach.

Thoughtfully-constructed syllabi and "test blueprints," which are discussed later in this chapter, are two of several possible approaches to connecting grades directly to desired course goals.

Grades and grading practices can be a component of formative assessment as well. For example, many faculty members use drafting and revising processes to teach writing. Students mimic the "real world" by writing multiple drafts, submitting them to critiques by the professor or their peers, and revising them for resubmission. Each draft may be assigned a grade in association with critical comments. Depending on the instructor's preferred strategy, all or only some of the interim grades may be used to determine the final grade. In this case, the grade for each draft, in conjunction with critical comments, gives the student an indication of his or her performance, what might be done to improve the product, and how the quality of the product changes over time.

Grading can be formative when there are multiple means and formats for assessing student learning and when there are repeated opportunities to demonstrate improvement within the context of one class. For instance, a professor might assign two or three papers (with required drafts), two class presentations, two objective format exams, and a journal that must be reviewed repeatedly by the professor during the semester. Each of these "assessment events" could be graded, providing students with at least two distinct types of opportunity to learn more or learn better. A student can compare his or her performance on the various assessment formats, thereby learning which skills he or she has mastered and which should be improved. In addition, a grade on the first test administration or the first paper or presentation serves as feedback (a formative assessment) that provides information on how to improve. This learning experience can be applied toward adapting study skills or work habits before the next attempt.

Self-report Measures

Concerns are often expressed about the use of self-report measures for answering questions about student learning. Sometimes these concerns relate to the use of indirect methods of assessing student learning and the concerns about qualitative versus quantitative assessment discussed previously. Often, however, concerns are related most directly to the validity and reliability of self-report measures. Self-report measures can be designed to be valid and reliable and can be assessed by applying the characteristics of reliability and validity described above.

Both common sense and face validity should be used to determine the value of a specific self-report measure. For example, if the goal is to determine whether students are satisfied, it seems that a self-report measure is the only means of gathering such data. Satisfaction, by definition, is one's feeling of liking, comfort, and fulfillment resulting from a specific event or situation. Similarly, it is appropriate to gather data on affective states (emotions) and social perceptions with a self-report instrument (assuming that it meets the criteria for reliability and validity).

It is possible to collect direct evidence of student learning using self-report measures, but these must be designed carefully to elicit evidence of student learning. For example, students may be asked to reflect on the most important thing they learned in a specific course, or what else they would like to learn on the same subject. In doing so, they would reveal the actual content of what they had learned. However, self-report questions such as, "Did you learn a lot in this class?" would not elicit such information. Self-report measures are most frequently used to provide valuable indirect evidence of student learning.

Statistical versus Practical Significance

Data related to student outcomes are often described as being "statistically significant" or "not statistically significant." The concept of statistical significance relates to the probability of a given result occurring by chance. If the result is too unlikely to have occurred by chance, it is said to be statistically significant.

For example, imagine two groups of students, each of whom has completed an introductory calculus course. Assume that members of each group were randomly assigned to two different teaching formats—one problem-based and the other traditional lecture—and that the same professor taught each course. At the completion of the course, both students are given the same standardized calculus examination. The average grade for the students in the problem-based course was 10 points higher than the average grade for the students in the traditional lecture course. Is a 10-point difference enough to make the claim that the problem-based course is a better form of teaching? Would a 2-point difference have been enough? Would 20 points be enough to make the claim? A test of statistical significance would reveal whether the 10-point difference could have happened by accident in a normally distributed population of students (i.e., the difference could have been caused by other factors, unrelated to the course, of which we are unaware), or whether the 10-point difference was large enough that in all likelihood it was caused by differences in the courses.

Judgments of statistical significance only become reliable when there are sufficient numbers of student test or survey results from which to draw inferences about a population of students. In many cases, faculty members will be studying outcomes data from small groups of students or engaging in formative assessment for which ongoing improvement in a class or a program is the goal. In these situations, faculty and staff members should make judgments and introduce changes based on "practical significance." Do the students' scores, or their change in scores from one time to another, reveal a pattern or appear to be meaningful or informative enough to support changes in a course or program?

In general, when large-scale assessments are being used, or when standardized tests are administered program-wide or institution-wide, statistical tests should be used to analyze the data. Guidance may be found in social science, education, mathematics and statistics, and other departments on campus that use empirical methods.

Judgments of student outcomes based on practical significance are equally valid when the number of students being evaluated is small, when data are qualitative rather than quantitative, and when the purpose is to engage in formative assessment.

Key Questions When Choosing and Implementing Evaluation Instruments

One should ask several questions when choosing assessment instruments:

❏ Is the evidence provided by the evaluation method linked to important learning outcomes?

This is perhaps the single most important way to determine the quality of most evaluation tools and methods. Regardless of whether an evaluation instrument is standardized (previously published and tested for validity and reliability) or "home grown" (created locally for a specific purpose), it is important to ensure that the instrument is designed to provide evidence of the desired learning outcomes. In research design terms, this involves determining whether the operational definition (the aggregate instrument or items on the instrument) actually assesses the construct (the learning goal) that it is intended to assess (construct validity). For many standardized instruments, the intended purpose will be apparent immediately. A disciplinary test, for example, such as the American Chemical Society (ACS) test, evaluates students' knowledge of facts, skills, and procedures that should have been acquired as a function of the undergraduate curriculum in an ACS-accredited program. Subject-area Graduate Record Examinations (e.g., the psychology GRE) evaluate content knowledge in the respective disciplines they represent. Publishers of other standardized tests with other less readily obvious content will explain, in the test information materials, what the test is designed to assess.

It is important, however, not to assume that the linkage between every item on a standardized assessment instrument and the construct it is designed to assess will be readily apparent. Many standardized instruments have built-in reliability checks and so-called "lie-scales." Measures that are designed to evaluate affective and social development are especially likely to incorporate a series of questions that seem irrelevant, but that actually enhance the instrument's validity.

❏ Is a standardized instrument appropriate for the learning goals of the institution?

It certainly is not necessary to use standardized assessment instruments. In fact, for most learning goals, none will be available. Although a test created locally may not have the same statistical validity and reliability as a standardized instrument, its relevance to the specific learning goals in question may make it a more appropriate and effective instrument. A "test blueprint" (an outline that matches test items with the learning outcomes they are intended to assess) can be used to construct a test or instrument or to evaluate how well an existing "home-grown" instrument assesses key learning outcomes.

❏ Is the evaluation method appropriately comprehensive?

No assessment tool or method can assess *every* important learning outcome, but the best ones assess a comprehensive and/or representative sample of key learning outcomes. It is not financially feasible to use several published instruments to assess multiple outcomes, nor is it feasible to subject students to multiple tests or surveys. (The latter has its own measurement problems.) Regardless of whether an assessment instrument is standardized or specially created, it should be as comprehensive as possible.

❏ Are important learning outcomes evaluated by multiple means?

Few evaluation methods are perfect. It is important to triangulate around important learning goals, assessing them through various means, and through tests of various formats. For instance, a standardized test of disciplinary knowledge may be an adequate form of assessment of students' content knowledge of a discipline, but it may provide no indication of his or her preparedness to be a good practitioner in that discipline.

❑ Are the questions clear and interpreted consistently?

In addition to examining the correspondence between learning goals and the assessment measures being used, it is important to assess whether its "non-content" properties are adequate. For example, a test should not be culture-specific, its vocabulary and sentence structure should be at an appropriate level, and it should not contain ambiguous, unclear, or double-barreled questions (i.e., questions that actually contain two questions).

Questions should be phrased carefully to ensure meaningful responses. For instance, imagine that a targeted learning goal is that students' desire to engage in community service increases after exposure to a service-learning program. Imagine also the following two questions asked of a graduate:

> ❑ "On a scale of 1 to 7, how likely are you to participate in community service activity?"

> ❑ "On a scale of 1 to 7, how much influence did your community service during college have on your desire to participate in community service in the future?"

Both of these questions are indirect measures of learning or development, but only the second provides information that would help the institution to improve the service-learning program.

A specially created instrument should be reviewed by several colleagues and students to ensure clarity, and it then should be pre-tested by some students who have diverse backgrounds and characteristics in order to clarify ambiguous items.

❑ Do questions elicit information that will be useful for making improvements?

Questions should be designed so that, when possible, they yield responses that both evaluate an aspect of the educational experience and suggest options for improvement. For instance, a survey designed to evaluate student experiences with the Career Services Office should ask about perceptions of its efficacy:

> ❑ "On a scale of 1 to 7, how important was the Career Services Office in helping you find employment upon graduation?"

The instrument also should ask how the office might be improved. For example, the respondent might be asked to name the three most useful activities of the Career Services Office for helping students find jobs and to name three ways in which the functions of that office could be improved.

The concept of creating questions that are useful for making improvements can be applied to direct assessments of student learning as well. For instance, a complicated problem in a physics class can be divided into subsections to help the professor determine which content or skill areas need additional reinforcement.

❑ Does everyone interpret the responses the same way?

When assessments of student outcomes are subjective—that is, if they do not require discrete or quantifiable or unambiguous answers—it is important to develop a rubric (criteria used to score or rate responses) to ensure comparability of review. There should be collegial agreement on what constitutes acceptable, inadequate, and exemplary responses or performance for each assessment instrument to be used, whether it is a paper, a project, a presentation, or an artistic offering. A rubric created to reflect the agreement should be pre-tested by having colleagues independently score the same work samples to see if their scores are consistent. The strategy of inter-rater reliability can be used as well, by enlisting two or more colleagues to "grade" each student's work or performance.

❑ Do the results make sense?

It is important to use common sense when developing assessment instruments, designing a scoring system or rubric, or interpreting data resulting from assessment instruments. One would expect honors students to outperform other students on their senior theses presentations. One also might expect those same students to fare better in applying to graduate school, but not necessarily in being hired to entry-level positions in corporations. Students who have completed a general education sequence should score better on tests of general knowledge and skills related to specified general education outcomes than students who have not completed the sequence. Unexpected results should trigger further inquiry.

❏ Are the results corroborated by other evidence?

It is always important to use multiple means of assessment to determine if a particular learning goal has been met. It also is necessary to compare assessment results for related goals for student learning and even for goals that would be expected to be mutually exclusive. For instance, rubric scores for the writing quality of senior theses should be corroborated by students' grades in composition classes. Faculty ratings and students' self-ratings of performance should correlate with each other. Focus group results should support survey results on the same topic. Conversely, students who demonstrate an increased personal emphasis on wellness by their attendance at the gym and by participation in athletics should not be engaging in increased alcohol and drug consumption. The latter finding would warrant re-evaluation of the campus wellness program.

❏ Are efforts to use "perfect" research tools balanced with timeliness and practicality?

Although institutions will do their best to ensure that the research designs they use yield meaningful results, they should remember that assessment cannot wait for the perfect research strategy. Indeed, there probably is no perfect strategy. For the purpose of managing the quality and change of an academic curriculum, assessment is a form of systematic inquiry—i.e., "action research" or "applied research," based on the collection and analysis of data about student learning that is undertaken with the best knowledge and resources permissible and within the time available. The resulting information guides decision makers in choices related to the curriculum, faculty, the use of physical space, and other areas that may have an effect on learning.

❏ Is evidence gathered over time and across situations?

Assessment is not a once-and-done process. As students, faculty members, curricula, and teaching methods evolve over the years, even institutions with very positive assessment results should undertake repeated assessments to ensure that students are learning as effectively today as they were a few years ago. Because each evaluation technique has relative strengths and weaknesses, there is no single perfect assessment that will yield absolutely accurate information and that is relevant to every situation. In order to have support the findings that each evaluation yields, more than one assessment strategy should be used to corroborate findings.

❏ How much should be assessed?

Plunging immediately into assessing a large number of students on a full range of learning outcomes will overwhelm faculty members and institutional resources. It will produce an overwhelming amount of information that may be impossible to interpret or to use in enhancing a program. It makes more sense to begin with a more limited approach. For example, faculty members assessing student writing skills might gain more from a thorough analysis of a sample of 30 papers than from a more perfunctory review of 300, as well as by assessing only a few key goals.

Just as every possible outcome need not be measured, it is not necessary to collect data about each student's performance. The Commission is interested in the institution's ability to graduate students with appropriate knowledge, skills, and behavior, not in a demonstration that every student was tested. Meaningful and representative sub-populations (randomly chosen when appropriate) can provide the basis for demonstrating that students across the institution are achieving learning goals.

Evaluating Student Learning

> ➤ Use indirect measures to explain or support findings from direct measures.

> ➤ Choose the most relevant level for evaluation of the learning goals: institution, program, or course.

> ➤ Select quantitative or qualitative measures based on type of student learning goals.

> ➤ Ensure that grades are related directly to goals.

> ➤ Choose appropriate research design.

> ➤ Use formative assessment "mid-course" to improve teaching and learning.

> ➤ Use common sense: Is the result logical?

❑ **Are faculty and staff members who are knowledgeable about measurement serving as resources for developing assessment instruments?**

The work of assessing student learning is essentially systematic inquiry in the tradition of social science or evaluation research, with its attendant need for validity, reliability, control, analysis, and interpretation, to the extent that these are possible. Although everyone involved in the enterprise is an expert in the content base of what is being researched (i.e., teaching and interacting with students in a higher education setting), few are expected to be experts in conducting research. While much of the work of assessing student learning has a common-sense base, it is also true that meaningful analysis of student learning, especially beyond the course level, requires expertise. There are usually faculty members on campus who are trained as social science, education, or other researchers. They can conduct careful, meaningful research and can construct measures. These faculty members, who can be found in psychology, sociology, education, business, and other departments, may be enlisted

to serve as internal consultants, reviewers, statisticians, and mentors in the assessment process.

Easy-to-Implement Tools and Techniques

The assessment tools and techniques presented below yield useful information and are relatively easy to implement. They are not meant to be an exhaustive selection of tools but, rather, an overview of available options.

Rubrics or Rating Scales

A rubric is an instrument based on a set of criteria for evaluating student work. Rubrics help a professor or other evaluator to make explicit, objective, and consistent the criteria for performance that otherwise would be implicit, subjective, and inconsistent if a single letter grade were used as an indicator of performance. Rubrics delineate what knowledge, content, skills, and behaviors are indicative of various levels of learning or mastery. Ideally, "grading" rubrics are shared with students before an exam, presentation, writing project, or other assessment activity. Conscious awareness of what he or she is expected to learn helps the student organize his or her work, encourages self-reflection about what is being learned and how it is being learned, and allows opportunities for self-assessment during the learning process. Huba and Freed (2000) suggest that instructors consider involving students in the development of rubrics as a class progresses as a way of helping students to develop their own conceptions of what constitutes good and poor work. Both Huba and Freed (2000) and Walvord and Anderson (1998) offer extensive information on developing rubrics.

Figure 6 includes a description of the characteristics and components of rubrics. Huba and Freed (2000) present a thorough description of the uses and purposes for rubrics, along with a comprehensive primer on how to construct them.

There are four basic types of rubrics: simple checklists, simple rating scales, detailed rating scales, and holistic rating scales.

Figure 6

Criterion-based Rating Scales (Rubrics)

What is a rubric? A rubric is a criterion-based rating scale that can be used to evaluate student performance in almost any area. A rubric establishes the "rules" for the assignment (Huba and Freed, 2000). It contains *a priori* criteria for various levels of mastery of an assignment.

How is a rubric used? The person evaluating student performance uses a rubric as the basis for judging performance. Ideally, rubrics are available to students prior to their completion of the assignment so that they have clear expectations about the components of the evaluation and what constitutes exemplary performance.

What are some of the criteria that may be used within a rubric to evaluate student work? Criteria can include sophistication, organization, grammar and style, competence, accuracy, synthesis, analysis, and expressiveness, among others.

What are the components of a rubric? Huba and Freed (2000) describe the following elements of rubrics:

➢ Levels of mastery (e.g., unacceptable through exemplary)

➢ Dimensions of quality (see criteria above)

➢ Organizational groupings (macro categories for criteria)

➢ Commentaries (the junctures between levels of mastery and dimensions of quality; e.g., a description of the characteristics of an exemplary organization)

➢ Descriptions of consequences (components of commentaries that relate to real-life settings and situations).

Where can I see examples of rubrics and learn more? Walvoord and Anderson (1998) and Huba and Freed (2000) are both excellent sources of information about the characteristics of rubrics and how to develop them. They also provide examples of various forms of rubrics.

Simple Checklists. This form of rubric can be used to record whether the relevant or important components of an assignment are addressed in a student's work. For instance, a rubric might be used to assess whether a laboratory report contained required sections or whether a writing sample contained all of the assigned parts. A checklist of this sort is categorical, that is, it records whether or not a required aspect of an assignment is present, but it does not record quantitative information about the level of competence a student has achieved or the relative skill level he or she has demonstrated.

Simple Rating Scales. This form of rubric records the level of student work or categorizes it hierarchically. It is used, for instance, to indicate whether student work is deficient, adequate, or exemplary, or to assign a numerical "code" to indicate the quality of student work.

In most cases in which a numerical scale is used, it should contain a clear neutral midpoint (i.e., the scale should contain an odd number of rating points). However, survey designers should determine when this might not be appropriate. Occasionally, such scales are intentionally designed without a midpoint in order to force a non-neutral response.

Figure 7, an excerpt from an employee rating scale, is an example of a simple rating scale that does not provide information about the "value" of different points on the scale.

Detailed Rating Scales. Detailed rating scales describe explicitly what constitutes deficient, adequate, or exemplary performance on each criterion. Detailed rating scales are especially

Figure 7

Excerpt from a Simple Rating Scale

Employer's Final Performance Evaluation of
Knowledge, Skills, and Attitudes (KSAs)
of: _____

Dear Employer:

The College of Business Economics (CBE) understands the need for its graduates to be broadly trained and ready to perform immediately upon entering the job market, both as individuals and in teams. Therefore, its curriculum contains concrete, measurable, and attainable objectives throughout. As a result, each CBE graduate is expected to perform successfully in the following areas of Knowledge, Skills, and Attitudes.

Please rate your intern or employee's performance only on the areas that apply to his/her job.
The rating scale is: 5=Excellent; 4=Good; 3=Satisfactory; 2=Fair; 1=Poor; N/A=Not Applicable.

Excerpt:

COMMUNICATION: WRITTEN, SPOKEN, GRAPHIC, AND ELECTRONIC	5	4	3	2	1	n/a
1. Write articulate, persuasive, and influential business reports, proposals, and letters						
2. Make articulate, persuasive, and influential individual and team presentations						
3. Develop graphic, spreadsheet, and financial analysis support for position taken						
4. Display presentation skills						
5. Generate appropriate visual aids						
6. Use correct written structure, spelling, grammar, and organization						
7. Articulate another's viewpoint through verbal and non-verbal cue interpretation						
8. Resolve interpersonal and team conflicts						
9. Negotiate effectively						
THINKING: CRITICAL, CREATIVE, AND INTEGRATED	5	4	3	2	1	n/a
10. Use problem-solving techniques						
11. Use adaptable, flexible thinking						
12. Use critical thinking to produce comprehensive, supported, integrated conclusions						
13. Use creative thinking methods to produce ideas						
14. Distinguish fact from opinion, and critical from non-critical information						
15. Develop several workable solutions to a problem						
16. Show common sense						
17. Demonstrate continuous learning (learning to learn)						

Source: College of Business and Economics, Towson University, November 2001. Adapted with permission.

Some of the other characteristics that could be evaluated in the manner shown in Figure 7 include:

- ❑ Technology
- ❑ Ethics and Values
- ❑ Business Disciplinary Content
- ❑ Leadership, Entrepreneurship,

- ❑ Diversity - International and Demographic
- ❑ Practical Excellence
- ❑ Job Experience and Career Development

useful when several faculty members are scoring student work, because they communicate common performance standards and therefore make the scores more consistent. Detailed rating scales are useful to present to students when an assignment is given or at the beginning of a semester or even a program. They provide students with a clear description of what they are expected to learn and the criteria upon which their learning will be judged.

Figure 8 is an example of a rubric designed as a detailed rating scale.

Holistic Rating Scales. Holistic rating scales define deficient, adequate, or exemplary student work as an aggregate, by assigning a single score to a constellation of characteristics that have been fulfilled to a substantial degree, rather than rating each criterion separately. Holistic rating scales often are used when evaluating student work that may vary so widely in form and content that the same criteria may not apply to all. Capstone projects in an art program, for example, might vary so that they cannot all be judged using the same specific criteria. However, a faculty member could create a generic description of what constitutes exemplary work, adequate work, and so on, regardless of the medium or focus of the work.

Figure 9 is an example of a holistic rating scale.

Self-reflection

Asking students to reflect on what and how they have learned—in other words, to engage in metacognition—has several benefits. Student self-assessments give faculty members useful insights into the learning process, help students integrate what they have learned, and provide students with an understanding of the skills and strategies they need to learn most effectively. Classroom assessment techniques suggested by Angelo and Cross (1993) and other similar self-reflection strategies have the added advantage of taking very little faculty or student time. The student often is asked to write simply a phrase or sentence. Examples of self-reflection questions that might be a useful part of an assessment program are provided in Figure 10.

Ratings/Comments from Internship or Research Supervisors

Programs that place students in practica, such as internships, cooperative education, and student teaching assignments, usually require that the on-site supervisor rate the student on essential knowledge, skills, and attitudes. Such scales are relatively simple to construct (see Figure 7.) Because these experiences require students to integrate and use much of what they have learned in a program, these rating scales are evidence of what students have learned during the program. Brief comments from supervisors also provide valuable insights into the overall strengths and weaknesses of a program.

Placement Rates

For professional programs whose goals include preparing students for a particular career, the proportion of graduates who find positions in that career is important indirect evidence of whether students are learning essential knowledge and skills. If a large proportion of graduates from a teacher education program is successful in finding teaching positions, for example, it is likely that those graduates have the knowledge and skills that school administrators consider important for successful teachers. Similarly, if a program aims to prepare students for graduate study or professional programs—pre-medicine and pre-law programs are examples—the proportion of graduates who are admitted into graduate or professional programs is important evidence that students have learned what graduate programs consider important for success in their programs. Note, however, that placement rates alone do not provide insights into exactly *what* students are learning. Therefore, they are usually insufficient evidence of student learning if used alone.

Figure 8

Example of a Detailed Rating Scale

This scale is adapted from one used to evaluate a "book journal and review" for a cognitive psychology class. For the assignment, students were expected to read one full-length book, chosen from a list provided by the instructor and related to the content of the courrse but not included on the required course reading list.

The purpose of the assignment was to provide a basis for making connections between the course content, other professional or popular work in the field, and students' daily exposure to topics or situations related to cognitive psychology in their personal lives and in their other courses. A further purpose of the assignment was to enable students to develop skills in describing research in cognitive psychology to the lay public.

The assignment involved reading the chosen book during the course of the semester and keeping a journal of reflections related to the purpose of the assignment. Students also were expected to write a professional style book review (of the type that might appear in the *New York Times* Review of Books). The rubric is abbreviated for inclusion here.

	Unacceptable	Fair	Proficient	Exemplary
Book Journal				
Use of grammar and style to communicate ideas effectively	Grammar and style that interfere with a reader's ability to understand the ideas presented	Grammar and style adequate for the reader to grasp the main concepts presented	Grammar and style allow the reader to understand easily the concepts presented	Grammar and style enhance the reader's ability to understand the concepts presented, including nuances of thought; May provide a pleasurable reading experience
Engagement with the author's ideas	Author's ideas are simply repeated, indicating that engagement was at or below a surface level	Occasional discussion of the author's ideas, suggesting ability to engage	Frequent discussion and analysis of the author's ideas, including expression of well-supported opinions about those ideas, suggesting almost constant engagement	Rich, mature grasp of the author's ideas, coupled with analysis and synthesis with own ideas and ideas of other writers and scholars, suggesting constant and sophisticated engagement
Connections between the course and the book	Very few connections with course material	Sporadic but meaningful connections with course material	Regular and meaningful connections to course material	Continual connections to course material and sophisticated discussion of those connections
Connections between other experiences and the book	Very few connections with other experiences	Sporadic but meaningful connections with other experiences	Regular and meaningful connections with other experiences	Continual connections to other experiences and sophisticated discussion of those connections

Book Review

Grammar and form	Grammar and style impede understanding of the "plot" or thesis of the book; not consistent with the form of a professional book review	Grammar and style are adequate for the reader to grasp the "plot" or thesis of the book; the form is consistent with that of a professional book review	Grammar and style allow the reader to understand easily the "plot" or thesis of the book; closely adheres to the style and form of a professional book review	Grammar and style enhance the reader's ability to understand the "plot" and thesis of the book; indistinguishable from a professional book review
Communication of cognitive psychology concepts to the reader	Ignores the reader's perspective of the reader and/or communicates cognitive psychology concepts inaccurately or without scientific analysis	Sometimes considers the perspective of the reader and occasionally communicates cognitive psychology concepts well	Consistently addresses the perspective of the reader and commuinicates cognitive psychology concepts accurately and usefully	Engages the reader and "forces" the reader to be interested in the topic of the book; describes cognitive psychology concepts accurately and usefully

Test Blueprints

The creation of local examinations—"traditional" examinations at the course level, or comprehensive examinations at the program level—ideally begins by writing a test blueprint before developing the actual test questions. Often called a table of specifications, a test blueprint is a list of the key learning outcomes to be assessed on the test, with the number of points or test questions to be devoted to each goal.

An example of a test blueprint appears in Figure 11. Note that in a test blueprint, an essential learning outcome might be represented by questions worth a total of 20 points, while a lesser learning outcome might be represented by only 5 points.

The test blueprint itself is important evidence of the test's validity. When matched with test scores, it offers clear evidence of what students have learned because it covers all learning goals. One could say with confidence, for instance, that a student earning an "A" on the test has mastered all or most of the important learning outcomes for a course or a program.

Other Assessment Tools

Some other assessment tools may be valuable components of many successful assessment programs, but they are more difficult or time-consuming to implement than the tools suggested above, and they also may require significant financial resources to purchase or administer. Careful consideration is warranted to determine whether information yielded from these strategies justifies the time and effort they require.

Multidimensional or Comprehensive Tests

As most faculty members are already aware, valid and reliable tests can be very difficult to design, especially those meant to assess higher-order thinking skills, attributes, or values. Tests of this type should be administered, analyzed, and revised over several semesters to eliminate poorly written items and to ensure optimal quality. It is best to seek the advice of a colleague who is an expert in "tests and measurements" before embarking on the construction of a comprehensive test of multiple student learning goals. Several books are primers on test construction. At the very least, they will provide the reader with an overview of the best

Figure 9

Example of a Holistic Scoring Guide (For Critical Thinking)

by Facione and Facione

[Ed. Note: The criteria below are shown from the highest score to the lowest.]

4 Consistently does all or almost all of the following:

- ❑ Accurately interprets evidence, statements, graphics, questions, etc.
- ❑ Identifies the salient arguments (reasons and claims) pro and con
- ❑ Thoughtfully analyzes and evaluates major alternative points of view
- ❑ Draws warranted, judicious, non-fallacious conclusions
- ❑ Justifies key results and procedures, explains assumptions
- ❑ Fair-mindedly follows where evidence and reasons lead

3 Does most or many of the following:

- ❑ Accurately interprets evidence, statements, graphics, questions, etc.
- ❑ Identifies relevant arguments (reasons and claims) pro and con
- ❑ Offers analyses and evaluations of obvious alternative points of view
- ❑ Draws warranted, non-fallacious conclusions
- ❑ Justifies some results or procedures, explains reasons
- ❑ Fair-mindedly follows where evidence and reasons lead

2 Does most or many of the following:

- ❑ Misinterprets evidence, statements, graphics, questions, etc.
- ❑ Fails to identify strong, relevant counter-arguments
- ❑ Ignores or superficially evaluates obvious alternative points of view
- ❑ Draws unwarranted or fallacious conclusions
- ❑ Justifies few results or procedures, seldom explains reasons
- ❑ Regardless of the evidence or reasons, maintains or defends views based on self-interest or preconceptions

1 Consistently does all or almost all of the following:

- ❑ Offers biased interpretations of evidence, statements, graphics, questions, information, or the points of view of others
- ❑ Fails to identify or hastily dismisses strong, relevant counter-arguments
- ❑ Ignores or superficially evaluates obvious alternative points of view
- ❑ Argues using fallacious or irrelevant reasons, and unwarranted claims
- ❑ Does not justify results or procedures, nor explain reasons
- ❑ Regardless of the evidence or reasons, maintains or defends views based on self-interest or preconceptions
- ❑ Exhibits close-mindedness or hostility to reason

For further information, contact the authors at Insight Assessment (info@insightassessment.com; Phone: 650-692-5628) or visit the website at http://calpress.com/rubric.html for a reproducible version and instructions.

Figure 10

Student Self-reflection Questions
for a Course or Program

1. How do you feel about writing/teaching/biology/sociology/etc.?

2. What will you say to your friends about this course/program?

3. What suggestions would you give other students on ways to get the most out this course/program?

4. How do you feel about yourself as a writer/teacher/biologist/sociologist/etc.?

5. What are your strengths as a writer/teacher/biologist/sociologist/etc.?

6. What makes a person a good writer/teacher/biologist/sociologist/etc.?

7. What was the one most useful or meaningful thing you learned in this course/program?

8. What was your biggest achievement in this course/program?

9. In what area did you improve the most? What improvement(s) did you make?

10. What one assignment for this course/program was your best work? What makes it your best work? What did you learn by creating it? What does it say about you as a writer/teacher/biologist/sociologist/ etc.?

11. Describe something major that you have learned about yourself in this course/program.

12. List three ways you think you have grown or developed as a result of this course/program.

13. In what ways have you improved as a writer/teacher/biologist/sociologist/etc.?

14. What have you learned in this course/program that will help you continue to grow as a writer/teacher/biologist/sociologist/etc.?

15. What was your favorite aspect of this course/program? Why?

16. What goals did you set for yourself in this course/program? How well did you accomplish them?

17. If you were to start this course/program over, what would you do differently next time?

18. What strategies did you use to learn the material in this course/program? Which were most effective? Why?

19. What risks did you take in this course/program?

20. If you could change any one of the assignments you did for this course/program, which one would it be? What would you change about it?

21. What problems did you encounter in this course/program? How did you solve them?

22. What one question about this course/program is uppermost on your mind?

23. What would you like to learn further about this subject/discipline?

24. In what area would you like to continue to strengthen your knowledge or skills?

25. Write one goal for next semester/year and describe how you plan to reach it.

Figure 11

Example of a Test Blueprint

Educational Research Methods: Final Exam Outline

The final exam will consist of 25 multiple-choice items, each worth 2 to 4 points, and five short essay questions, each worth 3 to 5 points. The items will cover most of the concepts listed below.

Validity and Reliability (Up to 16 points)

❑ Demonstrate an understanding of reliability and validity.

❑ Correctly identify the type of reliability and validity evidence being provided by given information on an instrument.

❑ Recognize examples of measurement error in a given situation.

❑ Assess the meaning and implications of measurement error.

❑ Apply general principles for ensuring validity.

Inferential Statistics (Up to 16 points)

❑ Demonstrate an understanding of the concept of a null hypothesis.

❑ Select the most appropriate inferential statistics (t, F, or χ^2) for a given research situation

❑ Know the most common "cut-off" point that statisticians use in deciding whether two means differ statistically significantly from one another.

❑ Correctly interpret the results of t, F, and χ^2 tests as presented in research articles.

❑ Interpret the effect of standard deviation and sample size on the results of a statistical test.

Experimental Research (Up to 12 points)

❑ Interpret correctly the symbolic representations of experimental designs.

❑ Describe the benefits and limitations of each experimental and quasi-experimental design covered in class.

❑ Identify the appropriate research design for a given research situation.

Correlational Research (Up to 12 points)

❑ Demonstrate an understanding of regression and the use of regression equations.

❑ Understand what r, R^2, and partial correlations are and what they tell us.

❑ Understand what multiple regression analysis is used for and what it tells us.

Qualitative Research: Observation, Interviews, and Ethnographic Research (Up to 16 points)

❑ Describe and discuss qualitative research and its key characteristics.

❑ Identify the pros and cons of qualitative research.

❑ Describe the concept of a focus groups.

❑ Identify the pros and cons of focus group research.

❑ Understand the key principles in conducting focus groups.

❑ Define ethnographic research is and identify or describe examples of it.

Historical Research (Up to 10 points)

❑ Describe the need for historical research.

❑ Identify kinds of historical research sources.

❑ Recognize examples of primary and secondary resources.

❑ Understand how to evaluate historical research.

Content Analysis (12 points)

❑ Demonstrate an understanding of content analysis.

❑ Understand the pros and cons of content analysis.

❑ Recognize examples of different kinds of content analysis.

❑ Explain how to analyze content analysis data.

Multiple Units (Up to 6 points)

❑ Identify the most appropriate research method for a given situation.

questions to ask when seeking expert advice (Anastasi and Urbina, 1996; Haladyna, 1999).

Adding a published test to an assessment program will require time to identify, evaluate, and experiment with potential tests. Unfortunately, many published tests aimed at the higher education market offer limited evidence of quality (i.e., validity and reliability) and have been normed with relatively small groups of students.

It is most important to compare the test blueprint against the key learning outcomes of the course or program in question to see how well they match. A biology test that focuses on ecological concepts, for example, probably would not be appropriate as a key assessment instrument for a biology program that aims to prepare students for careers in health professions.

Figure 12 contains a list of published tests designed to test critical thinking and general education goals. It is presented here as an example of the various test characteristics that should be considered when choosing an appropriate published assessment instrument.

Ad Hoc Surveys and Pre-graduation Surveys

Many people view surveys as a quick way to collect assessment information. Unfortunately, surveys that are designed and administered quickly often have low response rates and poorly-phrased questions that yield information of questionable value.

Indirect assessments of student perceptions and satisfaction that are administered at the institutional level and are not embedded in course and program requirements—such as voluntary graduating senior surveys—take extra time and effort for both students and faculty members, and they present sampling problems. It also can be difficult to motivate students to participate in such extraneous assessment efforts, or to give their best possible effort and thought, thus reducing the validity of the assessment itself. It is often simpler, more efficient, and more effective to use assessment strategies that are intrinsic parts of course and program

requirements. Graduating senior surveys, for instance, could be administered as part of a capstone course offered in every major.

If an institution determines that a survey is a key element of an assessment strategy, it should help to ensure useful results by conducting a pilot test of the survey. A draft should be administered to a small group, the responses analyzed, and unclear questions identified. Strategies to maximize the response rate should be included in the plans to administer the actual survey.[5]

Focus Groups

A focus group interview often is viewed as another quick way to collect assessment information, but the relatively small number of participants and the free-flowing format can reduce the credibility and value of the results. Focus groups are usually most appropriate as tools to help illuminate other assessment results, rather than as stand-alone assessment strategies.

Successful focus groups require time for planning, testing, and analysis to ensure a balanced discussion among a sufficient number of participants and to assure that the results have credibility and value. One should learn how to plan and conduct focus groups, hire a consultant, or enlist the aid of an on-campus expert before using focus groups as an assessment strategy.

Several sources introduce the science of conducting focus groups and their use as a source of information. For example, see Morgan (1997); and Krueger and Casey (2000).

Portfolios

Portfolios are structured, focused, and purposeful collections of student work. They are increasingly popular assessment strategies, because they provide an exceptionally comprehensive, holistic picture of student learning.

Figure 13 offers some questions that may help in a decision on whether or not to use portfolios. If the decision is made to use portfolios, it is best to start on a small scale. Portfolios may be especially

---

5 For a discussion of effective survey use, see Suskie (1996).

Figure 12

Commonly-administered Measures of Critical Thinking

Measure	Critical Thinking Definition	Subscales	Design	Appropriate Participants
Watson-Glaser Critical Thinking Appraisal	Comprises attitudes, knowledge, skills	Inference, Recognition of assumptions, Deduction, Interpretation, Evaluation of arguments	Parallel forms A & B; 80 multiple-choice items, based on readings; 40 mins. to complete	9th grade and higher
California Critical Thinking Skills Test	Purposeful, self-regulatory judgment	Analysis, Evaluation, Inference, Inductive, Deductive	Parallel forms A and B; 34 items; 40 mins.to complete	College age
California Critical Thinking Dispositions Inventory	Attitudinal inclination to apply critical thinking skills	Truth seeking, Open mindedness, Analyticity, Systematicity, Critical thinking self-confidence, Inquisitiveness, Cognitive maturity	Likert-type scale; 75 items; Response ranges from Agree to Strongly Disagree; 40 mins.to complete	College age
Ennis-Weir Critical Thinking Essay Test	Reasonably deciding what to do or what to believe	Getting the point; Seeing reasons and assumptions; Stating one's point; Offering good reasons; Seeing other possibilities; Equivocation; Irrelevance; Circularity; Reversal of conditional relationships; Straw person fallacy; Overgeneralizations; Excessive skepticism; Credibility; Using emotive language to persuade	Essay format; Responses written to questions about scenarios; 40 minutes to complete	Grade 7 to College
Cornell Critical Thinking Test	Reasonably deciding what to do or believe	Level X: Induction; Deduction. Credibility, Assumptions, Value judgment; Meaning Level Z: All level X subscaled plus semantics, prediction, definition	Level X: 71 multiple- choice items based on scenarios; Level Z: 52 multiple-choice items based on scenarios; 50 mins. to complete	Level X: 4th grade-college sophomore Level Z: gifted high school and college-aged adults

References: Adams, M., Whitlow, J., Stover, L., and Johnson, K. (1996). Critical thinking as an educational outcome: An evaluation of current tools of measurement. *Nurse Educator, 21 (3),* 23-31.

Facione, N.C. (1997). *Critical thinking assessment in nursing education programs: An aggregate data analysis.* Millbrae: The California Academic Press.

Ennis, R. H. & Millman, J. (1985). *Cornell critical thinking test, Level 2.* Pacific Grove, California: Midwest Publications.

Ennis, R. H. & Millman, J. (1985). *Cornell critical thinking test, Level X.* Pacific Grove, California: Midwest Publications.

Rane-Szostak, & D. Robertson, J. F. (1996). Issues in measuring critical thinking: Meeting the challenge. *Journal of Nursing Education, 35(1),* 5-11.

Note: This table contains information on the most commonly used measures of critical thinking only. It is not meant to be exclusive. There are many more measures available, including several domain-specific measures. Table prepared in 2001 by D. A. Redding,Ph.D., Instructional Assistant Professor, Mennonite College of Nursing, Illinois State University. Reproduced with permission..

appropriate for programs that enroll only a handful of students. Such programs would be ideal for piloting portfolio projects for later use with larger programs.

Portfolios can present significant logistical problems related to sampling, storage, development of evaluation criteria, and the allotment of sufficient faculty and staff time for review. These issues can be resolved, but the solutions may take time to identify and implement. For example, a number of institutions use electronic portfolios to solve the storage problem. Huba and Freed (2000) provide an excellent discussion of the development and assessment of portfolios.

Retention/Graduation Rates

Retention and graduation rates that do not meet the institution's goals may be signs of problems with student learning. However, they do not necessarily reveal what students actually have learned. They can be useful to the extent that they correlate with and illuminate direct learning assessments, or that they assess directly such institutional outcomes as cost effectiveness, diversity, student achievement, and other evaluations of institutional effectiveness.

Figure 13

Considerations when Deciding to Use Portfolios

1. What are the goals of the portfolio?
   - ❑ What do you want your students to learn by the act of creating a portfolio?
   - ❑ What processes or outcomes are to be evaluated by the portfolio?

2. How will students choose what to include in the portfolio?

3. How and when will work be inicluded in the portfolio?

4. How will student and faculty reflection occur in the portfolio process?

5. How will the portfolios be reviewed and evaluated? What would a successful portfolio in your program look like? What are your criteria for deciding if a portfolio is a "success"?

6. Will the portfolios be graded? If so, how?

7. How and where will portfolios be stored?

8. Will the portfolios be passed one faculty member to another? Will students retain ownership of portfolios?

9. What are the benefits of moving toward portfolio assessment? What are the areas of concern?

10. Is the collection of student work a feasible practice in your program?

4

The Student Learning Assessment Plan in the Context of Institutional Planning

The focus on student learning assessment and institutional assessment in *Characteristics of Excellence* places both forms of assessment within the context of institutional mission and institutional strategic planning. Although student learning and institutional assessment are addressed in separate accreditation standards (Standards 7 and 14), each is an integral part of the other. The emphasis is placed on all assessment as a cohesive process, not as a static or special event or an *ad hoc* exercise occurring just before accreditation evaluations.

The most important reason that all assessment should be an ongoing process is that it is conducted primarily for the institution's benefit and only secondarily for outside constituencies like accreditors. If an institution is making its assessment practices work to improve student learning, the expectations of accrediting agencies will be satisfied in the process.

Because assessment is for the institution itself, and because it grows out of the institution's own mission, the Commission does not specify a one-size-fits-all model of assessment, nor does it dictate the form an assessment plan should take or the specific learning goals that are set within the context of the plan. Each institution "owns" its assessment plan (see the Context section of Standard 14). Therefore, it is the responsibility of the institution to decide what type of assessment

should be performed, in what sequence, within what time frame, and for what result.

The institution's plan for the assessment of student learning may be included as a component of its overall institutional assessment plan (Standard 7), or it may be a separate document that is incorporated by reference in the institutional plan. It also can feature plans created by separate units.

The model shown in Figure 15 illustrates the basic relationship of the assessment of student learning to the larger institutional environment.

The goal of the present chapter is to provide guidance and a framework to help institutions to develop assessment plans within the context of overall institutional assessment and strategic planning:

✦ The first section of the chapter discusses the institutional planning context in which plans for the assessment of student learning are developed and implemented.

✦ The second section presents characteristics of effective plans for assessment.

✦ The third section describes the components of a typical institutional plan for assessment of student learning.

✦ The fourth section describes student learning assessment plans at the course and program levels.

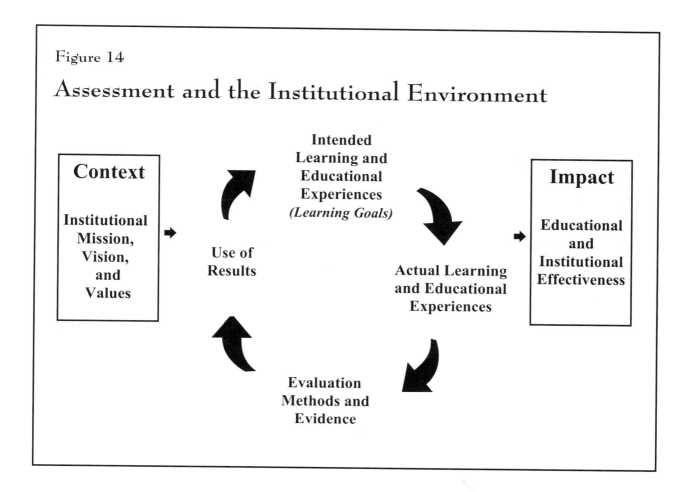

Figure 14

Assessment and the Institutional Environment

Context

Institutional
Mission,
Vision,
and
Values

Use of
Results

Intended
Learning and
Educational
Experiences
(Learning Goals)

Actual Learning
and Educational
Experiences

Impact

Educational
and
Institutional
Effectiveness

Evaluation
Methods and
Evidence

The Commission does not expect institutions to use the material presented here as a required template for crafting a plan. The structural and institutional examples presented are intended to be resources to aid institutions in developing their own unique plans.

Assessment of Student Learning within an Institutional Context

Excellent institutions are self-reflective and continually seeking to improve. The Commission has long challenged its member institutions to pursue excellence, and it understands that the purpose of outcomes assessment is twofold: accountability and improvement. External forces and internal priorities require institutions of higher learning to demonstrate their effectiveness and efficiency to students and to the broader public. The improvement of overall educational quality and the enhancement of effective teaching and learning

will occur when faculty and administrators work together to implement a sound, institution-wide program of outcomes assessment (Standard 7: Context).

The Commission expects institutions to have developed and implemented an assessment plan or plans that focus on the overall effectiveness of the institution and its constituent programs and functions. To this end, each of the 14 standards includes a fundamental element relating to the assessment of that standard. Seen in this context, the assessment of student learning is one component of the institution's overall assessment, albeit the most important one.

This handbook focuses primarily on the assessment of student learning, but many of the characteristics that apply to the assessment of student learning apply equally to the assessment of other aspects of the institution, and the general structure for assessment plans presented later in this chapter can be easily tailored to assess "non-academic" goals of an institution.

Before discussing the structure of a plan for the assessment of student learning, it is important to explore several characteristics that express the synergy between the institution's efforts to ensure desired student learning outcomes and its planning process.

Mission serves as the foundation for all planning.

The institutional strategic plan, the institutional assessment plan, and the associated plan for the assessment of student learning should all acknowledge and draw on the mission, vision, and values of the institution as their defining context. Institutional mission ensures that each leads the institution toward the same goals and that the plans do not work at cross-purposes with one another, thereby fostering competition for scarce resources. More generally, the Commission's standards connect the assessment of student learning with institutional assessment to assure that "institutional processes and resources support appropriate learning and other outcomes for students and graduates" (Standard 7).

Assessment plans are aligned with the institutional strategic plan.

Student learning should be the fundamental or core goal of every institution of higher education, and overall strategic planning efforts should be directed ultimately to the enhancement of student learning. It is important, then, that the strategic plan takes into account the assessment plan and that results from student learning are used to inform the strategic plan.

For instance, a specialized institution preparing students for careers in the applied sciences may discover that its students learn best in active rather than passive learning situations. Active learning may require more square footage allocated to laboratory and clinical space, whereas passive learning may require more lecture space. Therefore, a strategic plan that provides for additional instructional space and a facilities master plan that includes additional lecture hall space will not be serving the needs of that institution's students.

The synergy between strategic planning and outcomes assessment planning is articulated clearly in Standard 7, which states that "[E]vidence gathered about students' development and learning outcomes can be used to make judgments about resource allocation in planning for overall institutional effectiveness and to enhance academic programs. Institutional effectiveness also is assessed to monitor and improve the environment provided for teaching and learning and for enhancing overall student success. Therefore, the assessment of student learning should be aligned with that plan and its constituent parts."

The strategic plan includes a plan for institutional assessment that provides for regular assessment of all of the institution's components and functions, particularly its overall effectiveness in:

- ❑ achieving mission and goals
- ❑ implementing planning
- ❑ resource allocation
- ❑ institutional renewal processes
- ❑ efficient use of institutional resources
- ❑ leadership and governance
- ❑ administrative structures and services
- ❑ institutional integrity
- ❑ assuring that institutional processes and resources support appropriate learning and other outcomes for its students and its graduates

An institution may choose to have each administrative unit develop its own plan for self-assessment, relating back to the relevant standard in *Characteristics*, or it may choose to develop an overall plan that accounts for each area or standard. The Commission urges institutions to choose whatever model fits most appropriately within the institution's context.

Assessment of student learning interacts with and informs self-assessment of other institutional areas.

Because student learning is a fundamental goal of every institution of higher learning, **the Commission expects a separately identifiable written plan for the assessment of student learning, although no particular form is required.** The student learning assessment plan may be a compilation of departmental plans, and it may be summarized in the self-study.

However, the plan operates in concert with the assessment of other aspects of the institution. The information gained through the assessment of student learning informs the assessment of other institutional areas. For example, suppose that the chemistry department discovers that its students are weak on laboratory skills, and it is determined that the quality of the instrumentation is poor, or perhaps lab sections are too large for students to receive the attention they need. This information can be considered in creating strategies for resource allocation by asking, "Are resources that should be directed to academic programs being directed to areas less important to institutional mission?"

Similarly, student affairs staff may discover that first-year students are not participating voluntarily in campus activities. Consequently, staff may determine that the institution's strategy of housing all first-year students together is not conducive to developing a sense of community. These assessment results will aid the residence life program in revising its housing strategies.

The campus community participates in creating and implementing plans.

Strategic plans, institutional assessment plans, and student learning assessment plans should be developed through a collaborative process that engages the campus community at all levels and involves all stakeholders. Of course, different stakeholders will assume leadership for different parts of the planning process, and the intensity of involvement of different stakeholder groups will vary. In every case, however, general input should be sought before a plan or even its major conceptual bases are complete, and there should be opportunity for comment from the broad campus community. In the case of plans for the assessment

of student learning, as discussed below, faculty leadership and participation is essential.

Once plans are formalized—or adopted by the governing body, in the case of the strategic plan—they should be continuously available for reference, and their contents should be familiar and meaningful to stakeholders.

Characteristics of Effective Assessment Plans

There are several universal characteristics of effective institutional and student learning assessment plans. They can serve as a guide and provide criteria for institutions to evaluate or revise their existing assessment plans. These characteristics apply to plans for the assessment of student learning at both the institutional and program levels; to a great extent, they are also applicable to plans for assessing other aspects of institutional effectiveness.

The plan acknowledges already existing assessment practices.

To the extent that prevailing institutional culture and practice support assessment, new assessment activities should be built upon existing practices. There will be many faculty members, library and information literacy professionals, and student affairs staff members who are already creating well-defined learning goals and linking them to effective means of assessing student performance. By using existing assessment, the institution can "start with success" to reinforce successful practices.

Conversely, if an institution's culture or processes are an impediment to constructive assessment activities, the culture or processes should be reconsidered.

The plan is created by a participatory process.

The best plans for assessing student learning are created as a result of a participatory process that involves faculty members and professional staff as the primary participants. Students also can offer valuable contributions at the institutional, program, and course levels. A shared governance structure that provides for faculty leadership in the development of curriculum and educational goals can serve as the basis for developing an assessment plan. Standing governance structures with strong faculty and professional staff participation and strong administrative leadership (at the vice president or provost level) can serve as incubators for an assessment plan.

A plan that grows from an established participatory process will be more likely to garner the respect of campus constituencies and much less likely to be viewed as a process that is imposed "top-down." An existing governance structure need not actually implement the plan. Rather, it may serve as the body that formulates and charges an assessment committee which will create and execute the plan, or it may serve as an advisory board to an assessment director. However a campus chooses to create and implement its plan, it should ordinarily work within its existing governance structure and campus culture and observe accepted campus conventions for beginning or implementing initiatives.

The plan is simple.

A simple, clear plan with a focused institutional mission, values, and priorities will be most effective. A simple plan is (1) directed at assessing the most important goals for student learning, (2) easy to interpret, (3) easy to implement, and (4) easy to adapt. Plans that are cumbersome, complicated, and difficult to understand are those that are least likely to succeed.

The plan is systematic.

To be systematic means that all important student learning goals are included in the assessment plan and that the plan recognizes the various domains in which student learning occurs.

A good plan also should provide for the systematic assessment of those goals. Systematic plans do not lead an institution in many different directions at the same time, but they do take into account the necessity to use several assessments that bear directly upon the learning goals in question.

Systematic plans are characterized by thoughtful and thorough evaluation methods. They should provide the basis for developing specific institutional, programmatic, and course level plans that are interrelated. As a result, there will be

evidence of continuity, coherence, and integration among levels (Standard 14: Context).

Plans should address appropriate learning categories and topics of student learning in association with the total range of educational curricula at the institutional, program, and course levels, as well as those involving other educational activities and related support services.

The Commission's standards do require that assessment plans address learning goals at various levels, but the standards do not require a parallel three-tiered approach to outcomes assessment (Standard 14: Context). In other words, to engage in systematic assessment does not mean that the same evaluations must be used at each level, or be repeated every year, or be applied to every student individually.

The plan has a realistic timetable.

The execution of an assessment plan is not a short-term proposition. It takes time to develop learning goals statements and to gather, analyze, and interpret information, to make decisions, to implement improvements, and to evaluate their effectiveness. These last two steps are the most critical part of the assessment process in that they make the assessment activity meaningful.

A plan that is overly ambitious in terms of its timetable may fail because it seems impossible to implement. The timetable should take into account the academic year and its "down-times," the strategic planning cycle of the institution, and the campus committee structure and its associated processes and protocols. It should include time within the cycle to effect improvements. Most importantly, the plan should consider the quality and content of the learning experiences it is designed to evaluate. An institution that puts considerable emphasis on general education goals, for instance, should not emphasize provisions for the assessment of student learning before the student has had meaningful exposure to the general education program.

A plan need not require immediate assessment in all areas. Assessment may be phased in to build on existing and accumulating assessment processes.

The plan is supported by institutional resources.

The Commission is aware that the increased emphasis on evaluating and enhancing student learning may require increased institutional resources as well as strong and consistent leadership. Although *Characteristics* does not specify what resources an institution should have, it does specify that "the human, financial, technical, physical facilities, and other resources necessary to achieve an institution's mission and goals are available and accessible" (Standard 3). Therefore, it is important that institutional resources are available for assessment planning, implementation, and sustaining assessment activities over the long term.

The cost of conducting assessment programs depends on the assessment methods selected, whether new instruments are developed or existing instruments are used, how results are processed and reported, the size of the institution, the scope of various assessment studies, and any faculty or staff development or support that is necessary. The list of factors will vary greatly among institutional types and among state systems of higher education.

Institutions might expect to incur costs in the following areas when developing and implementing assessment programs:

- ❏ personnel costs

- ❏ constructing new or purchasing existing assessment instruments

- ❏ administering instruments, conducting interviews or focus groups

- ❏ data entry and analysis

- ❏ computer hardware and software

- ❏ communication costs for organizing efforts and for reporting and disseminating results

Other secondary costs include those related to faculty and staff time needed to design and implement assessment plans at all levels.

The plan makes wise use of faculty and staff time.

Institutions that carefully consider the budgetary implications of new or expanded initiatives often fail to recognize the resource implications for faculty and staff time. Thoughtful assessment is a time-intensive process that deserves prominence when prioritizing faculty time. It is directly and inseparably linked to teaching and mentoring and therefore should be considered part of a faculty member's load, rather than being treated as an "add-on" or as part of institutional service. Faculty members may need reassigned or release time to plan, execute, and communicate assessment activities and results and then to plan improvements. Faculty and staff members should be encouraged to take advantage of professional development activities, including on-campus workshops and attendance at professional conferences. Some institutions may consider offering small grants for exemplary projects that reflect outcomes that the institution values. Incorporation of assessment activities into teaching load and time and support for professional development and improvement usually are incorporated into a good assessment plan. It is reasonable to expect that the definition and assessment of student learning will become less time-consuming as they become more familiar.

Components of Institutional-level Plans for the Assessment of Student Learning

Comprehensive plans for the assessment of student learning at the institutional level take into account the institution's mission and provide for the manner of assessing student learning at the institutional, program, and/or course levels with varying degrees of specificity, depending on the nature and size of the institution, institutional governance and procedural conventions, institutional culture, and the level or levels at which the institution has chosen to conduct assessment.

Some institutions may incorporate department and programmatic assessment plans into their institutional assessment plans, most will delineate at the institutional level broad principles, goals, and characteristics by which departments, programs, and other units can develop their own subsidiary plans. These plans then can be appended to the institutional assessment plan. This approach affords the opportunity for departments to take responsibility for their own plans and for those closest to the students to make decisions about what students should be learning.

Figure 16 lists each component of a plan for the assessment of student learning in the left column. In the other two columns, it further describes those components as they fit within the plan at the institutional and program levels.

The Commission does not expect institutions to adopt the format or structure described below and presented in Figure 15, but most good institutional plans for the assessment of student learning will contain these or similar components in some form.

Institutional mission

As a cornerstone of the plan for the assessment of student learning, the college or university's mission provides a context for developing goals for student learning. It helps to keep the focus where it should be—on the main goals of the institution—and away from less meaningful goals that may sidetrack and unnecessarily complicate the assessment process. It should appear at the beginning of the plan to remind readers that it serves as the foundation for the plan.

Description of the relationship among the institution's strategic plan, institutional assessment plan, and student learning assessment plan

The first section of this chapter discussed this relationship in greater detail, but the purposes of including student learning assessment in the institutional assessment plan are to (1) make public and transparent the relationship among an institution's various planning and assessment activities, (2) prevent overlap and the unnecessary duplication of effort and resource allocation, and (3) formalize the process by which information about how students are learning will affect institutional planning.

Guiding Principles

This section of the plan sets forth guiding principles for how assessment is conducted on campus. The institutional level plan includes principles for both the institutional and department or program level. The set of principles for the latter level can serve to unify departmental assessment practices without prescribing a particular content for those plans. The use of guiding principles allows for flexibility in approach for each program. For instance, depending on the nature of their disciplines, departmental faculty may rely more heavily on qualitative rather than quantitative measurement or standardized measures more than campus-developed measures.

Principles should be developed with the institutional culture in mind and should respect intact policies and processes. Some examples of guiding principles include: (1) assessment focuses on key learning goals, (2) assessment processes are participatory, (3) time lines are reasonable, (4) sufficient resources are devoted to meaningful assessment activity, (5) assessment tasks are shared, and (6) assessment is conducted in a non-threatening environment.

Process for setting learning goals

The plan should describe how learning goals are to be developed, in order to ensure that goal development is not arbitrary or idiosyncratic. The process might include, for instance, a review of existing goals, an analysis of past student performance, or a review of the performance of students from peer institutions. If relevant, this section of the plan should articulate the standing processes and structures in place for developing or adopting goals.

Conceptual relationship of learning goals at different levels

The plan should describe, in broad terms, how learning goals at the departmental level fit within the context of learning goals at the institutional level. For instance, the plan should specify whether general education goals are viewed as institutional level goals or programmatic goals, and how general education goals are supported within major programs. Chapter 2 includes a detailed discussion of the relationship between learning goals and several resources for developing goals.

Figure 15

Components of Student Learning Assessment Plans At the Institutional and Program Levels

Subject	Institutional-level Plan	Departmental or Program Plan
Mission	Description of how learning goals will relate generally to institutional and departmental mission	Description of how learning goals will relate generally to institutional and departmental mission
Relationship between plans	Description of how the strategic plan, institutional assessment plan, and plan for the assessment of student learning are related conceptually*	Description of how the departmental assessment plan relates to the institutional plan for the assessment of student learning; how course-based assessment practices fit with the plan in general
Guiding principles	Description of guiding principles for conducting assessment on campus, at all levels	Description of guiding principles for conducting assessment at the department level (in addition to those described in the institutional plan) and at the course level
Process for setting learning goals	Description of the process for developing institutional student learning goals	Description of the process for developing programmatic learning goals
Conceptual relationships of learning goals at different levels	Description of how, conceptually, institutional learning goals are related to departmental and programmatic goals	Description of how, conceptually, departmental and programmatic goals are related to institutional-level goals and course goals
Learning goals	Definition of institutional level learning goals	Definition of departmental and programmatic learning goals
Assessment methods	Choice of assessment methods and rationale	Choice of assessment methods and rationale
Reporting and using results	System for regular sharing of results and for effecting change based on results	System for regular sharing of results and for effecting change based on results
Time line	Time line consistent with institutional assessment and strategic planning time line	Time line consistent with institutional assessment time line
Responsibility for enacting the plan	List of who (what office, group, or individuals) will be responsible for enacting the plan	List of what individuals or groups will be responsible for enacting the plan
Process for reviewing the plan	Description of how the institutional assessment plan for student learning will be reviewed and revised	Description of how the departmental or programmatic plan for student learning will be reviewed and revised
Provision for resources	Provision for funding, staff, and/or other support for enacting the plan	Description of resources and staff necessary to accomplish the plan

* This involves a description of the form that various institutional plans will take. For instance, will the plan for institutional assessment be part of the strategic plan document, or will it be separate but related? Will the plan for the assessment of student learning be part of the institutional assessment plan document, or will it be separate but related?

This section of the plan should be specific enough to allow campus stakeholders and other readers of the plan to understand how goals at various levels relate to one another. It should not be overly detailed, however, and should not include exhaustive descriptions and complicated matrices of hierarchies of goals. Materials such as these, if developed, should serve as a resource for those conducting assessment, not as a direct component of the plan.

Articulated goals for student learning at the institutional level

This is the most important aspect of the institutional asessment plan. Chapter 2 of this handbook is devoted entirely to the formation of learning goals, and the reader is referred there for resources on developing goals. This part of the institutional plan for the assessment of student learning should include the process by which goals are developed and a description of how various units of the institution work together to provide students with learning experiences that contribute to institution-wide goals. For example, an institutional goal to educate global citizens may be the responsibility of the academic departments, the residence life program, the student affairs program, the library and information resources staff, and the general education program.

There are no clear dividing lines among goals at the institutional, programmatic, and course levels, nor is there isolated responsibility for achieving them. Thus, programs contribute to institutional level goals, and courses contribute to programmatic goals. For almost all institutions, it would be futile to attempt to articulate all of these relationships in a one-to-one fashion, accounting for each and every goal and delineating the overlap so that the three levels fit together like a jigsaw puzzle. Nor would complicated matrices that define these relationships necessarily be the best way to conceptualize the relationship between goals. Instead, students probably would be best served if those devising assessment plans focus on the big picture, asking: How can our goals for student learning be meaningfully articulated, accomplished, and assessed? For example, general education skills are taught at all levels; the focus should be on whether they have been learned, rather than on what level.

If administrators, faculty, and librarians, student affairs staff, and students are familiar with the institution's mission, with goals at other levels, and with the guiding principles set forth in the assessment plan, those responsible for assessment at each level can be charged with developing and assessing goals relevant to that level. The institutional-level plan, then, need not delineate specific learning goals at the program or course level. The plan can, however, include guiding principles for how department and program faculty and staff can create their own plans for the assessment of student learning at the program and course level, including expectations about deadlines for presenting assessment results and how departmental-level assessment data can inform institutional assessment.

Assessment methods used to evaluate the attainment of those goals

This section of the plan should delineate how the goals for student learning will be assessed and who will take responsibility for evaluating them. Chapter 3 of this handbook is devoted to the evaluation of student learning, and the reader is referred there for resources devoted to this topic. The institutional plan for the assessment of student learning is not likely to include detail on how these evaluations are carried out but, rather, provides a framework and general description of how the institution is going to answer the question: "To what extent are our goals for student learning being achieved?"

At the institutional level, common measures and methods would be used for all students, although the variety of methods used will depend on the goals being evaluated and other factors, including budgets available for purchase of commercial testing instruments. Departmental or programmatic evaluation methods would be included in the assessment plan for the particular department and could vary considerably, depending on department need.

Process by which assessments results are reported and used to improve student learning

The assessment of student learning does not stop when the data are collected. An assessment plan should articulate in broad terms the processes that are used for determining whether the learning experience needs to be changed and, if so, how it should be changed. Even summative assessment, used at the end of a course or program to assess "final" learning, should be used to help revise curricula. Otherwise, assessment becomes a meaningless exercise. Chapter 5 of this handbook focuses on strategies and models for using assessment results, and the reader is referred there for an in-depth discussion of this topic.

The plan might include a provision for standing committees on curricula, general education, student affairs, and strategic planning to discuss assessment results on a cyclic basis and to make recommendations for change. For instance, a college may have a general goal for students to learn to appreciate diversity. The responsibility for achieving this goal may be college-wide, but perhaps a large portion of the diversity programming is carried out by residence life staff and instructors in first-year general education courses. Assessment results—perhaps gleaned from focus groups or student self-reflective writing—may indicate that students do not, in general, have the appreciation for diversity that was expected. Those charged with reviewing assessment results use these data to explore the possible reasons that the goal was not achieved and to then make recommendations, through an accepted process, to change programming or perhaps broaden the responsibility for achieving the goal.

It is important to note that the process described here is for institutional change, related to the attainment of institutional-level goals for the assessment of student learning. An analogous process would occur at the department level for programmatic goals.

Time line or cycle for enacting the assessment plan

The time line or cycle for enacting and maintaining the assessment plan should fit effectively within the institutional assessment and strategic planning cycles so that each of these processes can inform the other. The time line for the plan also should be reasonable and not overly ambitious. The goal is to provide enough time to complete each phase of the plan and time to make careful, deliberate decisions about any curricular or other changes that might take place as a result of the knowledge gained through assessment. Decisions about deadlines should never be arbitrary or *ad hoc*; this only reduces enthusiasm for assessment activities.

Delineation of responsibility for enacting and maintaining the plan

The individual(s) responsible for leading an assessment effort should be identified and the scope of their responsibilities articulated. Ideally, leadership of assessment should occur within the context of the standing governance structure. If an individual leader—either a faculty member or administrator—is appointed, provision should be made for regular communication and interaction between that individual and campus governance committees, academic departments, and co-curricular units of the institution.

Process by which the institutional assessment plan is periodically reviewed

An assessment plan should be practical and effective. Ineffective plans are likely to be of little use in the ultimate goal of improving student learning, and they are likely to promote exasperation with and rejection of the assessment process and the concept of assessment in general. One way to ensure that the plans are effective is to build an evaluation process and schedule into the plan. The process need not be complicated or cumbersome. If a cyclic review of assessment results by various constituencies is in place (see above), the evaluation of the plan itself can be incorporated into that process on a regular basis.

Provision for funding and support for enacting the plan

The resources needed to support the plan should be identified, and there should be a strong and clear connection between the scope of the plan and the resources available to sustain it. For instance, commercial standardized tests can be quite expensive, especially if the intention is to administer them regularly to the entire student body. Such tests should not be a component of the plan if the institution does not have the financial resources to purchase them. Similarly, planners should consider how much time faculty and staff members can devote to assessment and whether the plan can provide for re-assigned time for key faculty members.

Assessment of Student Learning at the Program, Department, and Course Levels

Departmental and programmatic assessment plans will follow a format similar to the institutional assessment plan described in the previous section of this chapter. Although plans for individual departments and programs will appear similar in overall structure—because they each will adhere to the same overall principles—the content of the plan, the learning goals, and the means used to evaluate them may be very different for various departments. For example, student learning goals for philosophy majors may focus more on critical thinking and ethical decision-making, whereas student learning goals for modern language disciplines may focus more on fluency of communication, ability to express oneself in the language, and perhaps an appreciation for the culture the language represents. The goals for these two programs would be assessed through dramatically different means and would require different emphases on qualitative and quantitative and direct and indirect measures. Nevertheless, the assessment plans of both programs would express the guiding principles for departmental assessment set forth by the institution (e.g., goals developed through a participatory process or procedures in place for using assessment results).

A typical departmental assessment plan will reflect a different level of assessment and a different place within the overall institutional assessment structure from an institutional plan.

Figure 15 gives examples of components of departmental or programmatic assessment plans and relates them to assessment at the institutional level.

Only a few of the areas of departmental program planning require expansion here, because most were described in the preceding section on institutional planning.

General description of the plan and departmental/programmatic guiding principles for assessment practices

Faculty members and students in a specific department may want their programs to have additional guiding principles for assessment practices that are particular to the program or to the departmental culture, over and above institutional principles. For example, a department may choose to protect junior faculty members from the work of departmental assessment outside of their own courses, choose to include students on departmental assessment committees, or commit to using national goals for student learning in the disciplines that have been developed by professional societies or learning goals related to professional accreditation as a cornerstone of their departmental or programmatic goals.

Description of the general relationship between departmental/programmatic and course level goals and assessments

The relationship between the assessment of student learning at the program and course level is analogous to the relationship between the assessment of student learning at the institutional and programmatic levels. Some courses, particularly those that are required of all students in the program, will have goals that directly correspond to goals at the program level. For other courses, the relationship may not be as direct. Several courses, for instance, may contribute to the development of critical thinking in the discipline or preparation for a career in the field. These interrelationships may prove too complicated, and may lose their meaning, if faculty members strive to have every course assessment directly related to a specific programmatic assessment. It may be more important to have faculty members articulate, in a general way, how each course contributes to the attainment of programmatic goals. These relationships between course and program should be described in the plan, as they provide the basis for determining which programmatic level goals are not represented in course work (or other programmatic activities like student research and internships). Faculty members then can seek to correct this imbalance by changing existing courses, adding new courses, or revisiting programmatic goals to see if they really are important for student learning. Chapter 2 includes a broader discussion of the relationship between course and program level goals.

Description of generally agreed upon course-based assessment practices

Faculty members maintain the responsibility for their own course-based assessments, and there will be myriad ways in which faculty in individual courses define goals and conduct assessments. The departmental/programmatic assessment plan is not meant to prescribe forms or methods of course-based assessment; instead, faculty members can develop a list of assessment practices and reach some consensus on which ones they value. This list of course-based values underlying assessment can serve as a guideline to help faculty members develop and improve assessment in their courses. One department, for instance, may value multiple-choice measures for their objectivity and may choose to encourage their use when appropriate. Another department may decide that a student's ability to express him or herself verbally is fundamentally important and that oral presentation should be assessed in some form in every course. Therefore, faculty would agree on the general form of assessment, but the department or program would not be dictating the specific form assessment would take in any individual faculty member's class.

Generally agreed upon course-based assessment practices are particularly important when several sections of one course are being taught by many different individuals or when much of the responsibility for course "coverage" is left to adjunct faculty.

5

Using Assessment Results
To Improve Teaching and Learning

A commitment to the assessment of student learning requires a parallel commitment to ensuring its use. Perhaps the most difficult part of assessing student learning is the process of effecting change in teaching and learning as a result of information gained through assessment practices. It is pointless simply to "do assessment"; the results of assessment activities should come full circle to have a direct impact on teaching and learning and on the institution's strategic plan to fulfill its mission.

Continuous improvement can occur in an upward spiral if an institution's structure is flexible, and if members of the campus community are committed to the assessment plan and are willing to integrate the results of assessing student learning into their collective vision of what the institution is doing well and what it could do better.

The first section of this chapter discusses the ways in which institutions can encourage the use of assessment results, the second section presents examples of specific types of change that might be made as the result of information gained in assessment, and the third section discusses the interconnectedness of assessment, teaching, and learning.

Institutional Support Strategies Designed to Encourage the Use of Assessment Results

An assessment plan will serve its purpose only if it provides for the use of assessment results. Regardless of the level at which assessment is conducted, an articulated plan for translating assessment results into changes in practice is essential. For such a plan to be effective, it requires an institutional commitment to the use of assessment results, the sharing of results, a broad campus discussion of and decision-making on those results, individuals who are empowered to make changes, the availability of resources for change, and flexible procedures for implementing changes.

An Institutional Commitment

The institution should demonstrate a commitment to developing a system for analyzing results, identifying areas of strength and weakness, creating a strategy for improving the learning experience, and implementing that strategy. Such a commitment will increase student learning as well as increase faculty and staff commitment to assessment. However, if the results of assessment are not used to improve student learning, assessment becomes at best a descriptive set of data about students and, at worst, a useless exercise.

Consider a business department that collects data regarding student or alumni performance on The American Institute of Certified Public Accounting Uniform CPA Examination and discovers that the majority of its graduates are failing the exam. This knowledge provides the opportunity to review the relevant parts of the curriculum, implement strategies for change, and gauge any improvement in student learning as a result of the changes made. In contrast, a tacit decision not to make curricular changes after discovery of this information could result in the demoralization of students and faculty, diminished stature for the program, and reduced selectivity in admissions.

Changes in programmatic curricula as a result of assessment data do not happen automatically, as many faculty and staff members can attest. However, if the department plan outlines specific procedures for examining assessment results and implementing curricular revision, those changes are more likely to occur.

Sharing Assessment Results

Assessment data collected at the institutional and program levels should be made available to the relevant members of the campus community. Data at the course level should be shared when it is appropriate to do so, such as when faculty members are collaborating to develop or revise a course, or are team-teaching a course.[6] When assessment data are collected but not shared with those who would be responsible for implementing change, the data are useless for practical purposes. Similarly, a perceived lack of faculty interest in assessment could be caused by the belief that assessment initiatives yield little or no meaningful information.

The first problem—when data are collected but not shared with those responsible for implementing change—can occur when one area or program collects data that are relevant to another area but fails to make the data available. For instance, social science faculty may assess their students' research performance via a required common paper, presentation, or capstone course. Assessments might reveal that students are not achieving desired

levels of information literacy. Students may fail to use analytical thinking when critiquing primary source articles, may cite materials improperly, or may conduct inadequate literature searches. This information can help in revising social sciences courses, but it also would be of great value to library staff members who design and deliver significant components of the information literacy requirement.

The second problem—when faculty members show little interest in assessment because they perceive it as meaningless—can result when data are collected at the institutional level to satisfy an outside agency, such as a state board of education or an accreditor, but are never shared with the faculty. In such cases, the failure to share data may be the result of hectic and unplanned-for data collection rather than an intentional withholding of important information from campus stakeholders. If there is no planned provision for collecting assessment data—for instance, if they are collected *ad hoc* to satisfy an external agency—there is unlikely to be a provision to share them regularly with the campus community.

There are cases in which an institution decides not to share data because it fears that assessment results indicating that students are not achieving desired levels of learning or that students are not satisfied will be shared with the general public and will impair the institution's ability to attract students. This is counter-productive for several reasons: silence by the institution about student performance is itself a red flag to the public, and poor performance by the institution's graduates will nevertheless be noticed by employers and the public. Most importantly, failure to share information with internal stakeholders precludes the opportunity to improve and to produce the type of student learning that will attract students to the institution. Even if an institution chooses justifiably not to publicize certain results externally, it should ensure that useful data are shared and used internally.

---

6 It is advisable to separate the assessment of student learning from the assessment of an individual faculty member's teaching, wherever possible, in order to encourage faculty members to engage in assessment activities, not to shun them.

For example, many institutions exercise their prerogative not to disclose to the public their results from the National Survey of Student Engagement (NSSE). The NSSE is a student self-report survey that measures what it describes as "student participation in programs and activities that institutions provide for their learning and personal development. The results provide an estimate of how undergraduates spend their time and what they gain from attending college."[7] In the NSSE, students report the number of hours they spent on schoolwork outside of class, the number of written papers completed, and the length of their papers, in addition to many other aspects of how they spend their time. Results such as these about student engagement can be invaluable to faculty members, librarians, and student affairs staff as they revise curricula and programs. Therefore, administrators and faculty members should give priority to the best interests of students by devising a system to share even sensitive assessment results internally, regardless of the test or measure from which they resulted.

Campus Discussion and Shared Decision-making

Assessment results are less likely to produce meaningful improvement in learning if only a small number of people or offices make all of the decisions about modifications to the learning experience.

Students should be included in discussions about assessment whenever possible, and they should be encouraged to engage in conversations with their peers about the institution's curricula and programs. Many campuses have specific courses or other learning activities that become the nexus of student complaints. For example, some general education courses frequently become the focus of complaints about a lack of "real world meaning" and connection to the major. Discussions about assessment results and curricular modification are an ideal venue to channel students' comments and criticisms constructively.

Empowering Individuals to Effect Change

Clear and public charges should be made to those who will be responsible for leading programmatic and curricular change that occurs as a result of assessment. At the course level, the individual instructor or group of instructors who teach a specific course would, of course, be responsible for its revision. At the program level, someone such as the department or program chair may be given the responsibility to ensure that change occurs. This person is often the same person who implemented the assessments. At the institutional level, however, several people from across the institution will be responsible for assessing and for changing the curriculum. For instance, the Office of Institutional Research might collect the data, and other offices or departments may be charged with effecting change.

It is important to articulate exactly who is responsible for change so that the data do not stagnate "on the shelf." For example, even if the office of career services is charged with conducting an annual survey on student acceptance rates at graduate and professional schools, it should be made clear which faculty members are responsible for implementing programs to improve education and increase graduate school acceptance rates.

Resources for Change and Celebration of Achievements

After assessment data are collected and curriculum and program revisions have been planned, resources must be available to implement the changes. Unfortunately, funds often are not available for every suggested change. Faculty members and administrators should review the institution's mission and strategic plan to determine funding priorities for new initiatives and to weigh the costs and benefits of proposed changes. A clear process for determining budgetary priorities should ensure commitment to the best interests of all students, rather than giving priority to the interests of a small group of faculty or students.

---

7 See www.iub.edu/~nsse/html/facts.shtml .

Assessment successes need to be positively reinforced in a way that makes the campus community aware of the value of assessment. Yearly celebrations can focus on effective assessment strategies, positive change as a result of assessment, or new assessment ideas. More importantly, traditional reward systems related to faculty evaluation, promotion, and tenure should take into account the valuable work of assessment.

Flexibility

This handbook has stressed the importance of well-communicated and clear procedures and plans for developing and implementing assessment programs. *Procedures, however, need not be arduous or cumbersome to result in positive change.* Inflexible and bureaucratic procedures discourage faculty from embracing assessment and adapting courses and programs in response to assessment results. For instance, engineering technology faculty members might decide that students need mini-practicum experiences early in their undergraduate careers because general student performance on senior projects is inadequate. Faculty are much more likely to modify the program to include early practicum experiences if their proposal is not stalled in committees. Institutions should strive to develop facilitative procedures that include relevant stakeholders and do their best to avoid bureaucratic structures that discourage change.

Translating Assessment Results into Better Learning

The most important reason for assessment is to ensure that students are learning. Even when the requirements of those to whom the institution is externally accountable—students, parents, legislators, and accreditors—provide the impetus for assessment, the fundamental expectation is that institutions of higher learning demonstrate that their students are learning.

Unfortunately, there are many obstacles to change. Faculty often object to performing yet another task related to assessment, citing additional demands on their time. They also might believe that the results of some assessment activities are invalid, or that the results demonstrate merely what the administration

wants them to demonstrate. Alternatively, institutions and committees may exhaust themselves planning for assessment and become "burned out" before results actually affect learning. Even when faculty members are committed to using assessment results to improve learning, the institution may not commit the necessary resources. It is common for accreditation teams to find beautiful assessment plans that have yet to be enacted, or "completed" assessment plans for which the resultant data sit on the shelf because the institution has not committed sufficient human or economic resources to support change.

Using assessment results need not be an onerous task, particularly for faculty who regularly adapt and modify their courses for the sake of their students. Using assessment results means changing courses or programs on the basis of real data rather than intuition. Even seasoned professors might be surprised by assessment data. Perhaps students are not reading a text because it is too elementary for them or too factual, instead of providing the type of analysis that might inspire their interest. Students who are performing extremely well on examinations nevertheless may not have been sufficiently challenged by the course. Perhaps students are performing poorly on one type of examination (e.g., an essay) because the mode of teaching was more conducive to performing well on another type of examination (e.g., multiple choice). The causes of ineffective learning experiences cannot always be explained by intuitive hunches.

Figures 17, 18, and 19 describe hypothetical and diverse ways of using assessment results at the institutional, course, and program levels. Although they are presented in a condensed and oversimplified form, they are not intended to imply that changing curricula, programs, or courses is simple or requires little thought. Rather, they are presented in the spirit of encouraging discourse among all members of the campus community, especially among faculty members and students. Each of the examples provides: (1) the initial learning goal at the institutional, course, and program level; (2) the measures or methods of assessing the goal; (3) the outcome evidenced by the measures; (4) the possible reason for the outcome; and (5) the action or actions taken as a result of the assessment.

Several noteworthy points are presented in these examples. First, the reader will notice that not all of the outcomes are "bad." Some of the examples indicate outcomes such as "students' projects demonstrate consistently high levels of quality." Examples of positive outcomes are used here to stress the point that when outcomes are "good"—that is, when students are meeting a learning goal—faculty members should consider whether the grade or the assessment reflect true competence, or whether the assessment or the goal is inappropriately easy and should be more ambitious. However, most of the examples here involve "bad" outcomes, because they provide an opportunity to think about the causes of poor performance and productive changes, not because outcomes in the "real world" are usually "bad."

The examples in Figures 16, 17, and 18 also illustrate the use of multiple assessments, direct and indirect measures, self-report and "objective" measures, and qualitative and quantitative data. Both direct and indirect measures are presented in the second column for many of the examples to illustrate the importance and interrelation of each. For instance, one of the examples presented in Figure 16 involves one direct measure (standardized writing tests) and three indirect measures (course registration statistics, transcript analysis, and course content analysis).[8] Other variations in form of measurement are represented in these examples as well. For instance, an institution seeking to produce students who compete well in the job market might use qualitative data (e.g., an alumni survey with open-ended questions) and quantitative data (an alumni survey with numerically-scaled questions, together with benchmarking statistics) to assess its goals. Faculty members may use quantitative and objective data (exam scores) and qualitative and self-report data (teaching evaluation comments) to assess the goal that students will master discipline-specific material. Most of these examples use multiple measures as well.

Finally, the "possible reason" or hypothesis for the outcome is presented as if it comes after the "measure" in time. This is not always the case. Often those who are focusing on the enhancement of student learning have developed several hypotheses before the assessments are administered; the assessment measures are used specifically to test the hypotheses. In these examples, the assumption is made that the measures listed are ongoing assessments that are part of a plan. The possible reasons for the outcome or hypotheses about what needs to be changed are drawn either from data gathered from the measures presented in the second column or from clearly related program or course characteristics—not at random or from intuitive suppositions.

For instance, one example in Figure 16 depicts two possible reasons for student dissatisfaction with a first-year community service requirement: the first is students' failure to understand the relevance to their chosen career or major, and the second is the time and transportation hardships students perceive. Both of these possible reasons for the outcome are drawn from data gathered in the first-year experience student satisfaction survey and focus groups, presented as measures in the second column. Another example, in Figure 17, describes students as having low fluency in modern language after having taken several courses. The hypothesis that lack of sustained and regular practice (i.e., infrequent class meetings) can be drawn from external research about optimum pedagogical practices in foreign language learning; it need not be drawn from a locally administered survey or test. Finally, the reader will notice that occasionally the "action taken" is to collect more data.

Appendix 7 offers a companion brainstorming exercise for which no likely causes or suggested actions have been specified. This exercise can be used with groups who are very new to assessment concepts. It allows for participants to draw on their own impressions and experiences in order to suggest how the faculty members and staff at the hypothetical institutions might proceed.

---

8 For an in-depth discussion of direct and indirect measures, their uses, and their advantages and disadvantages, see Chapter 3.

Figure 16

Using Assessment Results at the Institutional Level: Maintaining Mission and Achieving Vision

Learning Goal: Students will...	Direct & Indirect Measures	Outcome	Possible Reason or Hypothesis	Action Taken
Appreciate the importance of civic responsibility	* First-year experience student satisfaction survey * Focus groups	Students express strong dissatisfaction with a first-year community service requirement.	* Students do not see relevance to chosen career or major. * Students have time or transportation constraints.	* Introduce student/alumni-run seminars about how community service was relevant for them. * Include references and examples related to community service in general education courses. *Provide transportation, offer credit or work-study funds.
Exhibit competitive career potential	* Alumni survey * Data from benchmark institutions	Graduates' salaries five years post graduation are lower than those of students with comparable positions who attended other institutions.	* Students are not trained in salary negotiation. * Students are under-prepared relative to other institutions.	* Offer opportunities for mock interview and mock raise requests. * Survey employers to determine cause. * Change curricula as a result of employer survey.
Complete the first-year successfully	* First-year retention rates * General education course grades * First-year-experience student satisfaction survey * Exit interviews for non-returning students	A first-year retention problem is traced to poor performance in general education courses.	Poor writing or analytic skills of students entering the program impede performance.	Change course sequence to offer writing, critical thinking course first.
Complete the Honors Program successfully	* Honors program retention figures * Analysis of course availability and registration statistics *First-year-experience survey *Focus groups	An honors program has low internal retention.	* Not enough honors courses are available. * Courses are not judged to be significantly different from regular courses, students do not feel challenged.	Allow first- and second-year honors students to take upper-division honors courses for credit.
Exhibit independent learning	* National Survey of Student Engagement (NSSE) results * Student, faculty, and student affairs staff focus groups	National Survey of Student Engagement indicates that students spend very little time on academic work outside the classroom.	* Students work many hours per week for pay. * Students are not being challenged academically.	* Allow paid internships in area directly relevant to curriculum. * Revamp course syllabi to require more meaningful work outside of class.

Learning Goal: Students will...	Direct & Indirect Measures	Outcome	Possible Reason or Hypothesis	Action Taken
Demontrate high-level writing skills	* Standardized writing tests in first and third years * Course registration statistics * Transcript analysis *Course content analysis	Little difference between performance of first-year students and juniors on a standardized writing test.	* Students avoid elective courses with a large writing component. * Students have infrequent opportunities to receive feedback on their writing.	*Require "writing intensive" courses with multiple opportunities for feedback on writing.
Develop leadership skills	* Descriptive data from student affairs on activity participation * Student focus groups *National Survey of Student Engagement (NSSE) results	Student participation in campus governance is low.	* Students work many hours off-campus for pay. * Students believe that the student government organization is ineffectual.	* Consider course, internship, or apprenticeship credit for student government participation. * Examine governance structure to revise, if necessary, in order to empower students.
Develop proficiency in academic and scholarly research skills	* User activity analysis of library resources * Library usage survey	Analyses of user activity demonstrate overuse of non-academic databases in lieu of scholarly ones.	*Students are not being taught the value of scholarly sources relative to popular sources. * Scholarly journals and other resources are not widely available in the library.	* Develop a required information literacy program that includes, among other things, examples of erroneous conclusions drawn from reviewing inappropriate sources. * Examine library budget with the goal of making more appropriate resources available. * Enter consortia that make scholarly materials easily obtainable for students.
Demonstrate career-skill preparation and preparedness for job-seeking	* Career Services appointment logs and attendance records for Career Services programs * Alumni surveys	Very low numbers of students make use of career services programs.	* Students are not aware of the services or their value. * Students who have used career services report low satisfaction.	* Require brief introduction to career services at first-year orientation and again in junior level general education courses; include testimonials from students who have used the services. * Revamp career services program to ensure better attainment of its goals.

Figure 17

Using Assessment Results at the Program Level: Preparing Students for Future Success

Learning Goal: Students will...	Direct and Indirect Measures	Outcome	Possible Reason or Hypothesis	Action Taken
Be prepared for graduate and professional degree programs	* Departmental survey of graduating seniors and recent alumni * Data from benchmark institutions	* Student admittance rates to graduate and professional programs are low, compared to similar institutions' rates.	* Students are not being "coached" about the graduate school application process. * Students have not been exposed to experiences (e.g., undergraduate research) that enhance their chances of graduate school admissions.	* Enlist junior faculty members who have recently finished graduate school to develop a coaching program. * Incorporate a research, scholarship, or practicum requirement for students in a graduate or professional school "track."
Communicate competently in the major	* Scores on faculty-developed rubrics for final oral exam and final report in capstone course	* Student performance in capstone courses is poor, as measured by rubrics for oral presentations and written reports.	* Students are not receiving enough experience in communication in prerequisite major courses.	* Revamp departmental curriculum to require oral and written reports in every course. * Revamp syllabus of at least one required course to include multiple communication experiences.
Integrate competently knowledge and skills acquired in the major	* Departmental survey of graduating seniors * Grade distribution analysis of senior capstone course grades	* Survey results reveal that students think the capstone course is an "easy A." * Grade distribution reveals inflation.	* Capstone course is "watered-down" to account for a variety of previous course experience. * Capstone course does not demand true integration of previous learning.	* Change capstone course from a special-topics course to a course that requires an independent, integrative project. * Include a seminar component that makes students responsible for some of the course content.

Learning Goal: Students will...	Direct and Indirect Measures	Outcome	Possible Reason or Hypothesis	Action Taken
Exhibit fluency in a foreign language	* Scores on faculty-developed rubrics for oral presentation at end of intermediate-level courses * Standardized oral proficiency exam	Students in a modern language program exhibit low levels of fluency in the language when tested after having taken several courses.	* Courses are offered only two days a week. * Students have few opportunities for sustained practice in target language.	* Schedule courses for shorter periods, four or five days a week. * Introduce dedicated housing or separate floors for language students. * Place a fluent "graduate student in residence" in student housing. * Require a study abroad or immersion experience for language majors.
Demonstrate applied competency in the major	Scores on faculty-developed rubrics	Students' applied projects (e.g., design, engineering, fine arts) consistently reveal high levels of quality as evidenced by scores on rubrics designed to assess their efforts.	* Students are very well prepared for applied projects in lower-level courses. * Could students be challenged even more?	* Require students to submit their work to external conferences or scholarly undergraduate journals. * Engage upper-class students as mentors for lower-class students.
Demonstrate competence in academic subject areas in the major	Standardized disciplinary test	Standardized disciplinary tests (e.g., the ETS subject area tests, American Chemical Society Examination) reveal "spotty" or irregular command of the discipline.	* Curriculum requirements uneven (i.e., no required courses in some target areas). * Courses poorly designed or delivered in target area (i.e., no permanent faculty member in that specialty).	* A team of faculty reassess course content. * Full-time faculty create syllabi for and mentor adjunct faculty. * Evaluate need for additional faculty time. * Provide stipends for excellent faculty to "retool" to teach in those content areas.
Demonstrate practical competence in the major	* Rating forms completed by practicum supervisor * Self-rating forms completed by students	Students in nursing, education, or other programs requiring practicum experience are receiving lower than desirable scores from their supervisors.	* Lower-level courses do not provide "mini-practicum" experiences. * Students have not been made aware of the importance of practica. * Little guidance is provided at practicum site.	* Interact with on-site practicum mentors to brainstorm about reason for the problem. * Revise prerequisite courses to include short practicum assignments.

Figure 18

Using Assessment Results at the Course Level: Ensuring Learning

[Note: Two of the goals are repeated on this chart to illustrate both "positive" and "negative" outcomes.]

Learning Goal: Students will...	Direct and Indirect Measures	Outcome	Possible Reason or Hypothesis	Action Taken
Master course content	* Mid-term exam scores * Course evaluations	Subject mastery is inadequate, as demonstrated by low in-class exam scores.	* Students are not engaged with the subject matter. * Teaching format and exam format may not be compatible.	* Experiment with alternative teaching formats (e.g., problem-based learning, rather than lecture). * Create "test-blueprints" to acquaint students with expectations. * Analyze test format to determine if it is appropriate (e.g., Is an essay test being used when the material was presented as a series of facts requiring no analysis?) and change test format if warranted.
Master course content	* Mid-term exam scores * Course evaluations	Subject mastery is very high, as demonstrated by expecially high in-class exam scores.	* Students are engaged with material. * Teaching format and exam format are compatible. * Students are aware of what competencies are necessary. * But are students being sufficiently challenged?	* Experiment with increasingly more difficult exams to gauge more accurately students' potential. * Provide additional and especially challenging in-class or out-of-class assignments and assessment.
Exhibit discipline-specific writing skills	* Rubric-scored writing assignments * Course evaluations	Average writing performance is expecially high, as demonstrated by rubric-scored writing assignments.	* Writing was effectively taught in prerequisite classes and/or is taught well in the target class. * But can students be challenged more, or can the course focus on the development of other skills?	* Engage students as mentors for other students who need help with writing. * Encourage students to submit their work to on- or off-campus literary or scholarly outlets for student work.
Exhibit discipline-specific writing skills	* Rubric-scored writing assignments * Course evaluations	Average writing performance is unsatisfactory, as demonstrated by rubric-scored writing assignments.	* Students were not prepared well in prerequisite classes. * Students were not receiving enough practice and feedback in target class.	* Require writing assignments with feedback in prerequisite classes. * Require writing assignments with feedback in target class. * Target specific aspects of student writing and focus assignments on them.

Learning Goal: Students will...	Direct and Indirect Measures	Outcome	Possible Reason or Hypothesis	Action Taken
Think critically and analytically	* Commercially-developed critical-thinking test * Problem-solving exercises * Applications problems	Analytical skills/ critical thinking are weak, as demonstrated by poor performance on problem-solving exercises or application problems.	* Students have received little practice with these skills. * Faculty member has limited expertise in teaching these skills.	* Examine prerequisite courses for opportunities to engage in critical thinking, and revise appropriately. * Establish faculty-to-faculty mentor pairs, with each faculty member having expertise in an area the other lacks.
Demonstrate discipline-specific information literacy	* Rubric-scored term paper * Student survey or course evaluations	Research skills are weak, as demonstrated by poor performance on research term paper.	* Expectations for term paper were not clearly spelled out. * Appropriate search engines or sources were not available in the library. * Little practice with these skills on smaller assignments.	* Create a "blueprint" for the paper, clearly spelling out expectations. * Require an early non-graded first draft and provide feedback. * Examine library funding for possible reallocation. * Revamp required course to include several practice assignments drawing on scholarly research skills in the discipline.
Exhibit Oral Communication Skills	Rubric-scored oral presentation	Oral presentation skills are weak, as demonstrated by rubric-scored presentation.	* Prerequisite courses required little practice in oral presentation. * Students were not directly informed about the characteristics of a good presentation and/or the expectations for the assignment.	* Include an oral presentation component in early required courses with a comparable rubric for providing feedback. * Create teams of students to critique each others' presentations before they are presented to the whole class, and include safeguards to make this a non-threatening, critically constructive situation.
Exhibit Quantitative Skills	Faculty-developed mathematics test administered in an accounting class	Quantitative analysis skills are weak.	No appropriate prerequiste course is required.	Test students and assign them to a prerequisite course, if necessary.
Exhibit High Student Morale and Satisfaction to Support Learning	Teaching evaluations	There is dissatisfaction with course format, teaching style, and level of course difficulty, as demonstrated by teaching evaluations.	* Over-dependence on lecture format * Little direct explanation of the value of the course or material. * Few opportunities for students to apply course content. * Faculty member inaccessible outside classroom.	* Experiment in small ways with non-lecture format (i.e., problem-based learning, group projects, "inter- teaching" in which students are expected to explain the material to each other). * Include an interactive discussion of the value of the material during the first class period, and regularly use applied examples to support course material. * Reconsider office hours schedule, or offer students opportunities to schedule appointments outside of office hours.

A Message to Faculty Members:

The Interconnectedness of Assessment, Teaching, and Learning

In the final section of this handbook we depart from the third person and move to the first and second person in order to speak directly to faculty whose lives are so connected with students in the classroom and in other learning situations on a daily basis.

The staff of accrediting organizations or those who support accreditation by volunteering their services are very aware that an intense emphasis on student outcomes carries with it the danger of shifting the focus from teaching and learning to ill-considered data-collection. Therefore, the Middle States Commission on Higher Education advocates sincere attention to what faculty want students to learn; it does not advocate a "bean-counting" approach to assessment and improvement.

If you are convinced, on a theoretical level, that outcomes assessment is a well-intended and even a good thing, you may be thinking that you cannot possibly incorporate it into your classes, in your laboratories, or in your other pedagogical interactions with students. Yet, there are several strategies that can be accomplished without dramatic increases in faculty workload. Taken together, they can transform the way students learn.

The list presented in Figure 19 was developed from a collection of recent research and wisdom on when and how students learn best. Nine of the eleven items involve practices or characteristics that originate in individual classes. The two remaining characteristics are also directly related to the classroom. The list, for the most part, is self-explanatory, and some of these characteristics can be fostered with little change in a professor's existing practices.

Here we elaborate on several of the items on the list, with an emphasis on how you can make small changes by engaging in assessment.

➢ **Students learn effectively when they have opportunities to revise their work.**

If you currently do not grade multiple drafts of papers, projects, or lab reports, or provide multiple critiques of artwork or performances, consider taking at least one assignment and building in two or more reviews. On the earlier review or reviews, offer comments or grade with a rubric, but give students an opportunity to refine their work further before you assign a final grade. If necessary, consider making the project shorter or eliminating another graded assignment in order to provide time for the extra grading additional reviews will entail.

Another way to provide additional opportunities for students to revise their work is to initiate a system of peer review in which students share work with each other and review it according to pre-defined objective criteria.

➢ **Students learn effectively when they understand course and program goals.**

Human beings take in information and learn new things much better when they have a framework upon which to rest new ideas. For instance, as an expert in your field, you can read a scholarly article much faster than can a novice. From prior experience, you know why the material presented in the article is important or not, whether it is controversial, whether it adds significantly to the current knowledge base in the area, and whether it appears to be a reflection of solid theory in your discipline. Without such background, the contents of the article would be meaningless or at least not as rich. If your syllabus has no goals or objectives listed, you are providing your students with no framework to help them understand where the course fits in with other courses, how the skills they will be acquiring translate to other

Figure 19

Strategies to Improve Student Learning

There is increasing evidence that students learn most effectively when:

- They understand course and program goals and the characteristics of excellent work.

- They are academically challenged and encouraged to focus on developing higher-order thinking skills, such as critical thinking and problem solving, as well as discipline-specific knowledge.

- They spend more time actively involved in learning and less time listening to lectures.

- They engage in multidimensional "real world" tasks.

- Their learning styles are accommodated.

- They have positive interactions with faculty and work collaboratively with fellow students; all learners—students and professors—respect and value others as learners.

- They participate in out-of-class activities, such as co-curricular activities and service learning opportunities, that build on what they are learning in the classroom.

- Assignments and assessments are intertwined with learning activities and focus on the most important course and program goals.

- They have opportunities to revise their work.

- They reflect on what and how they have learned.

- They have a culminating "capstone" experience, such as a seminar, internship, independent study, research project, or thesis, that lets them synthesize what they have learned over the course of their college experience.

Sources:

Angelo, T. A. (1993, April). A "teacher's dozen": Fourteen general, research-based principles for improving higher learning in our classrooms. *AAHE Bulletin, 3* (7), 13.

Barr, R. B., & Tagg, J. (1995, Nov/Dec). From teaching to learning: A new paradigm for undergraduate education. *Change, 27* (6), 12-25.

Chickering, A. W., & Gamson, Z. (1987, July). Seven principles for good practice in undergraduate education. *AAHE Bulletin, 39* (7), 5-10.

Kuh, G. (2001, May/June). Assessing what really matters to student learning: Inside the National Survey of Student Engagement. *Change, 33* (3), 10-17, 66.

Mentkowski, M. & Associates. (2000). *Learning that lasts: Integrating learning, development, and performance in college and beyond.* San Francisco: Jossey-Bass.

Pascarella, E. T., & Terenzini, P. T. (1991). *How college affects students: Findings and insights from twenty years of research.* San Francisco: Jossey-Bass.

What research says about improving undergraduate education. (1996, April). *AAHE Bulletin, 48* (8), 5-8.

domains, or why they should be interested in the topic.

However, if objectives are listed, and they are made meaningful through a discussion of their importance and of the students' own objectives for the course, you will be modeling the behavior you use in your own scholarship. If you extend the discussion further and ask students to reflect on how class activities meet the objectives, you will be offering them a framework to evaluate all of their learning experiences, including those in other classes and in their future educational experiences.

> **Students learn most effectively when they (and you) reflect on what and how they have learned.**

If you have well-articulated goals for your course and if you have engaged students in a conversation about the importance of the course and its relationship to other aspects of their college program, the next step is to ensure that the pedagogical content of the course leads to achieving those goals. One technique that is not time consuming is to spend five minutes or so before each class listing the course goals or objectives for the class. Keep the record of your reflections for one semester, and at the end, look at it in aggregate. Are the goals supported relatively evenly? Is one goal over-represented (e.g., Is more time devoted to content than to process than seems appropriate given the goals)? Is there evidence that a large portion of time is spent on topics or activities that are not directly related to a course goal? Use the data you have collected to revise the course, perhaps only slowly over the course of several semesters, in order to help steer it toward the intended goals.

> **Students learn most effectively when assignments and assessments that are directly relevant to course goals are intertwined with learning activities and focus on the most important course and program goals.**

Consider an assignment that you give regularly or an exam format that you use most often. Does the assignment draw on or help teach the

particular capabilities that you are hoping to nurture in your students? Perhaps you assign a term paper each semester on a topic related to the subject area of your course. Is the sole purpose of the assignment to have students gain an in-depth knowledge of a particular topic? Do you have some tacit goals such as teaching students to engage in scholarly research, develop writing skills, or learn appropriate citation techniques—or is your goal simply to evaluate what they have been able to learn on their own? If these goals are tacit, rather than explicit, it is unlikely that your students will be aware of them, and thus unlikely that they will organize their work around them. If students are unable to connect the assignment to specific goals, the term paper is probably not an assessment of what they have learned in your class but, rather, an assessment of their "natural" competencies or characteristics, or prior learning.

In the case of examinations, many teaching faculty develop the habit of using the same format for exams over and over, without thinking of the congruence between what they want students to learn and the way they are assessing the learning. The format used for examinations may be the one that they found most congenial when they were students, the one that comes in a test bank with the text, or the one that is quickest to prepare or grade. However, every examination format has positive and negative characteristics.

For example, multiple-choice exams can be more psychometrically sound—more reliable and valid—if they are developed properly, than casually developed essay exams. Conversely, essay exams can sometimes allow for the assessment of a deeper, more synthetic (or analytic) exposition and certainly provide a venue for students to demonstrate their creativity or unique perspectives. Yet, no examination is valid if it is measuring something other than what it is intended to measure. Students frequently lament, "We didn't know what you were going to put on the exam" or "You didn't teach us the answers to the questions on the exam." These students may be more sophisticated and less lazy than they appear. What students really might be saying is that this particular class did not prepare them to take this particular exam.

Some students, nevertheless, perform exceedingly well. These students would be a useful group to shed light on the connection between the class and the exam. Do they feel they could have answered some of the questions without ever having taken the course? This can happen in the case of essay questions that involve the use of logic or synthesis more than they do course content, or for which course content could have been gleaned outside of class. Do high-performing students feel that they could have done well on a multiple-choice test simply by memorizing the content of a text? An instructor may deliver brilliant and engaging lectures, but if he gives an exam on the content of the text instead, he has no assessment of what students learned during those great lectures.

A brief look at your assignments and exams relative to your goals and the content of your class presentations can be accomplished in a very short period of time. Greater insight can be gained by conducting some 10- or 15-minute "focus groups" with students about the congruence between the course and the assessments. Any changes that appear to be indicated can be made one at a time or over the course of a few semesters.

> **Students learn most effectively when they understand the characteristics of excellent work.**

The debate about grade inflation is complicated, although most professors probably identify easily with a specific perspective. The first common perspective is that if we would all just use a normal curve to grade, we wouldn't have grade inflation. The second perspective is that if we didn't tie teaching evaluations to faculty tenure and promotion, we wouldn't have grade inflation. The third perspective is that grade inflation is not necessarily a problem. If we are teaching for mastery—i.e. achievement of learning goals—then many students will earn high grades. Without taking sides, it is easy to make the case that grades mean very different things to the outside world, depending upon who assigns them. In a curve system, no one except the professor knows anything about students'

absolute performance. Some professors probably do grade generously hoping to receive good student evaluations. Even when professors' grades are meant to indicate mastery, we do not know which student mastered the material as a result of the course and which student had already mastered it before her arrival. It is clearly beyond the scope of a handbook on student learning assessment to solve the complex problem of incongruence among professors' grading systems. However, regardless of your perspective on grade inflation and within the context of your own class, you can ensure that grades are meaningful so that students recognize the characteristics of excellent work. After all, it is what the student learns, not the grade itself, that is most important.

Test blueprints are one way to make grades meaningful (see Chapter 3). The professor plots out what it is that a student is expected to master, and the professor might even create a hierarchy of mastery tied to various grades. After a student takes an examination, she can go back to the blueprint and reflect on her grade relative to the concepts she was expected to have mastered.

Rubrics (see Chapter 3) make the grading process more transparent, more accessible, and when well formulated, they are diagnostic for the student (Walvoord & Anderson, 1998). In reviewing his rubric scores, a student can pinpoint his areas of strength and weakness and develop his own learning goals to strengthen performance in specific areas.

Another accessible way to make grades more meaningful, although less structured than a rubric, is to write relevant and instructive comments on student work, including multiple-choice exams! Surprisingly, most students find few comments on their work that provide meaningful feedback, relegating tests and assignments to the category of summative assessment. It does take longer to write comments, but if they are important and strategically placed, there needn't be many.

How could one write meaningful comments on a multiple-choice exam? Questions on these exams fall into several categories, including memorization (Did the student acquire necessary facts?); application (Given a scenario, can the student classify it, or extrapolate from it?); inference (If this happens, then what would happen?); and analogy (A is to b, as c is to d?). Students tend to err in patterns, frequently missing questions of the same type. Some guidance on which types of questions are causing difficulty for each student will almost certainly help him to focus his attention on the problem area next time.

As with the other areas discussed above, reflection on the meaning of grading—both the "score" and the comments offered—needn't take a great deal of time, and modifications in one's practices can be made gradually.

> **Students learn most effectively when their learning styles are accommodated.**

Recent pedagogical literature is replete with information about the varieties of learning styles that students can exhibit. Much of the work on learning styles has its genesis in traditional personality theory and its modern applied counterparts, such as the Myers-Briggs Type Indicator (Briggs-Myers, 1992), which classifies personality along four dimensions and yields sixteen types. Other heuristic impetus for work in the area of student learning styles comes from the theory of Kolb (1984) who defined four constituent processes involved in learning, Gardner (1983) who developed the now well-known concept of "multiple intelligences," and Sternberg (1988) who posited three distinct kinds of intelligence. Appendix 8 offers some background information on learning styles in the form of Frequently Asked Questions (FAQs) for those who are interested in exploring this topic in greater depth.

The focus of the learning styles approach as it applies to teaching is that all students learn differently, either because of their personalities or their diverse patterns of cognitive ability, and that teaching formats within a class should be equally diverse to accommodate students' learning needs. Because the most commonly used teaching method is the lecture-discussion format, some students with either personality types or learning profiles that prevent them from

assimilating easily information in this format may be learning less in the classroom than their counterparts who "prefer" such a format. This is an over-simplification of the learning styles approach, but the concept is not complicated. Different students learn best in different ways and in different settings, and failure to take this into account can impede learning in some students.

For a variety of reasons, we are not advocating that professors assess each student's learning profile and make associated individual accommodations (see Appendix 8). However, any instructor can diversify his or her presentation and the types of experiences associated with a specific class to increase the chances of engaging students who may not thrive in a lecture-based classroom. Knowledge about learning styles can be used to modify other aspects of a course as well. Hartman (1995) suggests that putting students together in groups to work on a project can have the best outcomes when students' learning styles are complementary, rather than similar. For instance, a group of students who all prefer theory or abstract thinking to concrete approaches may have difficulty organizing and getting started on the project, whereas another group of students, all of whom prefer detail and information- gathering over integration of ideas, may complete the project more efficiently, but may produce a less synthesized or mature product. Combining students with these styles will mix the best of both approaches.

In parting...

The purpose of defining goals and assessing learning is to improve learning through teaching. Teaching lies primarily in the hands of faculty members, and good learning cannot happen without their commitment and dedication. *Assessment, first and foremost, is a tool for faculty members to use as they do their very best to teach their students well.*

Appendix 1

Assessment Standards in
Characteristics of Excellence in Higher Education

Standard 7: Institutional Assessment

The institution has developed and implemented an assessment plan and process that evaluates its overall effectiveness in: achieving its mission and goals; implementing planning, resource allocation, and institutional renewal processes; using institutional resources efficiently; providing leadership and governance; providing administrative structures and services; demonstrating institutional integrity; and assuring that institutional processes and resources support appropriate learning and other outcomes for its students and graduates.

Context

The Commission on Higher Education expects institutions to assess their overall effectiveness, with primary attention given to the assessment of student learning outcomes, which are fundamental to the accreditation process. This standard on institutional assessment has a clear relationship to and builds upon the six previous accreditation standards, each of which includes periodic assessment of effectiveness as one of its fundamental elements. Information obtained through assessment should be used as a basis for assessing the institution's effectiveness in achieving its stated goals. In addition, outcomes assessment should be linked to an institution's ongoing planning and resource allocation processes. Consequently, evidence gathered about students' development and learning outcomes can be used to make judgments about resource allocation in planning for overall institutional effectiveness and to enhance academic programs. Institutional effectiveness is also assessed to monitor and improve the environment provided for teaching and learning and for enhancing overall student success. Assessment of student learning is addressed more particularly under Standard 14.

While the Commission expects institutions to engage in outcomes assessment, it does not prescribe a specific approach or methodology. The approach and methodology to be employed are institutional prerogatives and may vary, based on the stated mission, goals, objectives and resources of the institution. Nevertheless, an institution engaged in self-study or periodic review should provide evidence that the assessment of outcomes, particularly learning outcomes, is an ongoing institutional activity.

Outcomes assessment is not an end; it should be a means by which an institution utilizes data to improve teaching and learning and for overall institutional improvement. Therefore, it is essential that faculty, administrative staff and others be involved in the assessment process.

The Commission has long challenged its member institutions to pursue excellence, and it understands that the purpose of outcomes assessment is twofold: accountability and improvement. External forces and internal priorities require institutions of higher education to demonstrate their effectiveness and efficiency to students and to the broader public as well. The improvement of overall educational quality and the enhancement of effective teaching and learning will occur when faculty and administrators work together to implement a sound, institution-wide program of outcomes assessment.

Fundamental Elements of Institutional Assessment

Relative to this standard, an accredited institution is characterized by:

❑ a written assessment plan and process that meet the following criteria:

- a foundation in the institution's mission, goals, and objectives

- periodic assessment of institutional effectiveness that addresses the total range of educational offerings, services, and processes, including planning, resource allocation, and institutional renewal processes;

institutional resources; leadership and governance; administration; institutional integrity; and student learning outcomes

- support and collaboration of faculty and administration

- systematic and thorough use of multiple qualitative and/or quantitative measures, which maximize the use of existing data and information

- evaluative approaches that yield results that are useful in institutional planning, resource allocation, and renewal

- realistic goals and a timetable, supported by appropriate investment of institutional resources

- periodic evaluation of the effectiveness and comprehensiveness of the institution's assessment plan;

- use of assessment results to improve and gain efficiencies in administrative services and processes, including activities specific to the institution's mission (e.g. service, outreach, research); and

- a written institutional (strategic) plan that reflects consideration of data from assessment.

Optional Analysis and Evidence

In addition to the evidence inherent within or necessary to document the fundamental elements above, the following, although not required, may facilitate the institution's own analysis relative to this accreditation standard:

- ❑ review of all components of the assessment plan and an analysis of representative data/findings

- ❑ evidence of institution-wide assessment efforts (e.g. committee minutes or reports)

- ❑ analysis of how the assessment infrastructure supports the evaluation process

- ❑ review of reports or other evidence of student involvement in and satisfaction with academic support programs and co-curricular activities

- ❑ analysis of student satisfaction survey results

- ❑ analysis of teaching effectiveness evaluations, including identification of good practices

- ❑ assessments of student advising and service programs, with recommendations for improvements and evidence of action based on recommendations

- ❑ assessments of campus climate by faculty and staff, with recommendations for improvements

- ❑ assessment of faculty and staff development programs

- ❑ evidence of continuous improvement, as evidenced in administrative policies and procedures

- ❑ review of evaluations of special, mission driven programs or projects, with recommendations for improvement, and evidence of action based on recommendations

Standard 14: Assessment of Student Learning

Assessment of student learning demonstrates that the institution's students have knowledge, skills, and competencies consistent with institutional goals and that students at graduation have achieved appropriate higher education goals.

Context

Outcomes assessment involves gathering and evaluating quantitative and/or qualitative information that demonstrates congruence between the institution's mission, goals, and objectives and the actual outcomes of its educational activities. While not all of the impact of an institution on its students can be readily measured, the assessment of student learning is essential whatever the nature of the institution, its particular mission, the types of programs it offers, or the manner in which its educational programs are delivered and student learning facilitated.

The systematic assessment of student learning is essential to monitoring quality and providing the information that leads to improvement. Implemented effectively, the assessment of student learning will involve the shared commitment of students, administrators and academic professionals. The assessment of student learning has the student as its primary focus of inquiry. It is related to the assessment of institutional effectiveness, which is important as a means to monitor and improve the environment provided for teaching and learning (see Standard 7: Institutional Assessment). Because the purpose for assessing student learning is to help students improve and to maintain academic quality, the assessment measures chosen should be those that provide the students, faculty, and others with information about student learning that is specific; address questions that faculty and the institution care about; and are useful for assessing and enhancing academic quality.

The mission of the institution provides focus and direction to its outcomes assessment plan, and the plan should show how the institution translates its mission into learning goals and objectives. In order to carry out meaningful assessment activities, institutions must articulate statements of expected student learning at the institutional, program, and individual course levels, although the level of specificity will be greater at the course level. Course syllabi or guidelines should include expected learning outcomes. Moreover, institutions can be flexible in their approach to defining student learning at these different levels, such as repeating goals (some general education goals, for example) across programs or defining the goals at the institutional or program level as being a synthesis of the goals set at the program and course levels.

While the specific learning goals at each level (course, program, and institutional) need not be included in the assessment plan itself, statements of expected student learning must be available on campus to those planning or implementing assessment activities and to those evaluating the institution.
These learning outcomes should be interrelated, and their continuity, coherence, and integration among the three levels should be evident.

Although an assessment plan addresses learning goals at various levels, the assessment plan does not require necessarily a parallel three-tiered approach to outcomes assessment. The institution should specify those assessment measures, methods, and analyses that will be used to validate stated expectations for student learning. In addition, while the assessment of learning first occurs on an individual student basis within a particular course, institutions may select the level or levels at which they report assessment data.

At the course level, for example, grades are an effective measure of student achievement, provided there is a demonstrable relationship between the objectives for student learning and the particular bases (such as assignments and examinations) upon which student achievement is evaluated. The assessment of learning outcomes at the program or institutional level is likely to be reflected in an aggregation or a synthesis of course-level assessments, including capstone courses, and may incorporate data from such additional measures as professional licensure examinations. It also may be based on a representative sampling of learning outcomes or of students across the institution.

In developing their assessment plans, institutions should begin, of course, with those assessment measures already in place, such as course and program completion rates, retention rates, graduation rates, and job placement rates, as well as pre- and post-testing, scores on standardized tests, performance on licensing exams, graduate school performance, and studies of alumni and former students. Institutions also should consider developing new datasets related to learning outcomes. In all instances, institutions should utilize multiple approaches, which may be qualitative and/or quantitative, to demonstrate that graduates have achieved stated learning outcomes.

Assessment is not an event but a process and should be an integral part of the life of the institution. It is the responsibility of the institution to decide what assessment tasks should be performed, in what sequence, within what time frame, and for what effect. Not everything needs to be assessed each year. For example, the assessment of major programs might be tied to program review cycles, and the assessment of general education might proceed in a sequential fashion, assessing different sets of general education outcomes each year. Such institution-wide planning should provide a broad framework within which student learning may be assessed in ways consonant with disciplinary and institutional expectations.

Finally, and most significantly, a commitment to assessment of student learning requires a parallel commitment to ensuring its use. Assessment information, derived in a manner appropriate to the institution and to the desired academic outcomes, should be available to those who develop and carry out strategies that will improve teaching and learning.

Fundamental Elements of Assessment of Student Learning

Relative to this standard, an accredited institution is characterized by:

❑ articulated expectations of student learning at various levels (institution, degree/program, course) that are consonant with the institution's mission and with the standards of higher education and of the relevant disciplines;

❑ a plan that describes student learning assessment activities being undertaken by the institution, including the specific methods to be used to validate articulated student learning goals/objectives;

❑ evidence that student learning assessment information is used to improve teaching and learning; and

❑ documented use of student learning assessment information as part of institutional assessment.

Optional Analysis and Evidence

In addition to the evidence inherent within or necessary to document the fundamental elements above, the following, although not required, may facilitate the institution's own analysis relative to this accreditation standard:

❑ evidence of assessment approaches that derives from the institution's mission and which might incorporate such outcomes as cumulative learning, analytical and information skills, specific competencies, knowledge and cognitive abilities, student attitude development and growth, life skills, student activity involvement, and physical skills and techniques

❑ analysis of assessment results including

- where applicable, basic skills development programs

- subject area knowledge

- development of general education and lifelong learning skills

- attitudes and values that relate to the mission of the institution and to the programs of study

❑ analysis of direct and indirect indicators of student achievement such as persistence and graduation rates, student satisfaction and other evidence of student goal attainment, licensure examination results, alumni satisfaction and achievement, including consideration of parity of outcomes across different student groups

❑ analysis of results from a variety of assessment strategies, including standardized tests, local comprehensive tests, course-embedded assessment, self-reported measures, and portfolio assessment

❑ analysis of course, department or school reports on classroom based assessment practices and their outcomes, including grading approaches and consistency

❑ evidence that assessment findings are used to:

- assist students in the improvement of their learning

- assist faculty in the improvement of curricula and instructional activities

- assist in reviewing and revising academic programs and support services

- assist in planning, conducting and supporting professional development activities

- assist in planning and budgeting for the provision of academic programs and services

Appendix 2

Enhancing the Campus Climate for Assessment: Questions for Academic Leaders

What is your personal commitment to assessment?

❑ Are you sufficiently familiar with current thinking about the principles and practice of assessment?

❑ Are you comfortable with the concept of assessment? Have you worked through any reservations you have about assessment?

❑ Do you understand why assessment is important?

❑ Are you personally committed to sharing leadership of assessment with the faculty?

How do you stimulate interest in assessment?

❑ Do you promote assessment when you talk formally and informally with faculty, students, and staff?

❑ Do you sponsor consultants, speakers, and forums on assessment? Do you support these programs with your active presence?

❑ Do you explain to faculty, students, and staff how assessment findings affect major decisions that you and your colleagues make?

❑ Do you have communication channels with your campus assessment committee(s)? Do you actively use them to promote assessment?

How do you help provide the people who will help the campus focus on assessment?

❑ Do you see faculty vacancies as an opportunity to move substantively toward promoting a learning-centered environment?

❑ Do you give hiring preference to faculty applicants who have documented success in creating a learning-centered environment for their students and in using assessment to strengthen teaching and learning?

❑ Do you ask faculty and staff applicants to demonstrate their skills in promoting active learning and their skills in assessment?

How do you give faculty incentives to focus on assessment?

❑ Do you offer ample incentives for faculty and staff (e.g., promotion/tenure/merit considerations, reassigned time, budget supplements) to refocus their work in ways that promote a learning-centered environment and/or strengthen assessment?

❑ Are you promoting a learning-centered environment and strengthening assessment major goals for your institution?

❑ Are you promoting a learning-centered environment and strengthening assessment major goals for you personally?

❑ Do you require proposals for new programs to include plans for assessing student learning?

Continued on next page ➤

How do you provide the training to enable faculty to strengthen assessment?

❑ Do you encourage your faculty and staff to participate in campus and off-campus professional development programs on assessment?

❑ Do you alert your campus's teaching/learning center and/or assessment officer to faculty and staff needs for professional development on assessment?

❑ Do you fund faculty and staff travel to assessment conferences, institutes, and workshops?

How do you provide the resources to enable faculty to strengthen assessment?

❑ Do you give any special funding to programs that make the most progress in strengthening and using assessment?

❑ Do you provide both "seed money" and sustained or other special funding for initiatives that significantly strengthen assessment?

❑ Do you encourage your institution to give priority to fundraising for programs and activities that make assessment a priority?

❑ Do you encourage and honor faculty who seek grants for resources that will promote a learning-centered environment and strengthen assessment?

How do you help the faculty focus their time on assessment?

❑ Do you make assessment a focus of program reviews?

❑ Do you encourage departments to set department goals that contribute substantively toward promoting a learning-centered environment and strengthening assessment?

❑ Do you encourage and reward scholarship of teaching as a scholarly activity?

❑ Do you help faculty find the time for assessment initiatives by helping to minimize paperwork and by relieving them of less-critical responsibilities?

How do you encourage measurable outcomes of assessment endeavors?

❑ Do you track the number of programs that make major progress in strengthening assessment?

❑ Do you track the percent of courses/sections that use the most appropriate assessment tools and strategies?

❑ Do you track the percent of students who participate in the embedded assessments of higher-order thinking skills?

❑ Do you track resource utilization to see how well it supports assessment?

❑ Do you develop other key performance indicators for assessment?

How do you celebrate and reward assessment achievements?

❑ Do you announce noteworthy student and faculty accomplishments to internal and external constituents?

❑ Do you create celebrations of assessment achievements, consistent with campus culture?

❑ Do you provide special resources (e.g., revenue sharing) to those making extraordinary contributions to assessment?

Appendix 3

Assessment Practices Quiz

Mark a "T" next to those statements that accurately describe the Middle States Commission's views on assessment of student learning. Mark an "F" next to those statements that do **not** accurately describe the Commission's views on assessment of student learning.

1. _____ Published tests are always preferable to locally developed assessment measures.

2. _____ Class assignments can be used to assess the learning goals of academic programs.

3. _____ Tests with numeric scores are preferable to qualitative measures such as focus groups.

4. _____ Surveys of student satisfaction with a program are insufficient evidence of what students have learned.

5. _____ Every learning outcome of every course and program must be assessed.

6. _____ All students should be assessed to demonstrate the effectiveness of a course or program; a sample of students is inadequate.

7. _____ Goals should not be changed after they are selected.

8. _____ The same assessment measures should be used in every assessment cycle.

9. _____ Grades alone are not direct evidence of student learning.

10. _____ The primary purposes of assessment are to maintain accreditation and satisfy external stakeholders; therefore, it is appropriate to schedule assessment cycles so that they coincid with accreditation self-studies.

11. _____ The most effective way to create an assessment plan is to adopt the assessment plan of another institution.

12. _____ Assessment efforts should focus on what is learned in academic courses and programs; assessing what is learned in out-of-class activities is not important.

13. _____ Self-report measures can yield useful information about student learning.

14. _____ The assessment of educational effectiveness and the assessment of institutional effectiveness are not related.

Appendix 4

Key to "Assessment Practices Quiz"

1. *False*   Published tests are always preferable to locally developed assessment measures. [*Both published and locally developed instruments have pros and cons, and both may have a place in an assessment program.*]

2. *True*   Class assignments can be used to assess the learning goals of academic programs. [*Class assignments, especially in senior capstone courses, can be valuable sources of "embedded" information on how well students are achieving the major goals of a program.*]

3. *False*   Tests with numeric scores are preferable to qualitative measures such as focus groups. [*Qualitative and quantitative measures offer different perspectives to an assessment program, and both can be valuable.*]

4. *True*   Surveys of student satisfaction with a program are insufficient evidence of what students have learned. [*Student satisfaction surveys are not direct measures of student learning. They can, however, be informative indirect measures of learning.*]

5. *False*   Every learning outcome of every course and program must be assessed. [*Only the key learning outcomes of courses and programs need be assessed on a regular basis.*]

6. *False*   All students should be assessed to demonstrate the effectiveness of a course or program; a sample of students is inadequate. [*Samples can be cost-effective sources of information, provided that the samples are representative of all students, and the samples are sufficiently large so that the results can be generalized.*]

7. *False*   Goals should not be changed after they are selected. [*Goals should be modified whenever it becomes clear that revising them would improve the student learning experience.*]

8. *False*   The same assessment measures should be used in every assessment cycle. [*Assessment strategies can be implemented on a staggered basis and can be modified whenever it is clear that a new or revised strategy would be more useful.*]

9. *True*   Grades alone are not direct evidence of student learning. [*Grades alone do not tell us exactly what a student has and has not learned. The information upon which grades are based—tests, student papers and projects, and the like—are direct evidence of student learning.*]

10. *False*   The primary purposes of assessment are to maintain accreditation and satisfy external stakeholders; therefore it is appropriate to schedule assessment cycles so that they coincide with accreditation self-studies. [*The primary purpose of assessment is to improve student learning. Assessment should be systematic, continuous, and ongoing.*]

11. *False*   The most effective way to create an assessment plan quickly is to adopt the assessment plan of another institution. [*Although an institution may choose to adapt some of the features of another institution's assessment plan, each institution should develop an assessment plan that is tailored to its own culture, mission, and needs.*]

12. *False*   Assessment efforts should focus on what is learned in academic courses and programs; assessing what is learned in out-of-class activities is not important. [*Both in-class and out-of-class activities include valuable learning opportunities that should be assessed.*]

13. *True*   Self-report measures can yield useful information about student learning. [*Asking students to reflect upon their learning experiences can yield valuable insights into what they have and have not learned, especially their attitudes and values.*]

14. *False*   The assessment of educational effectiveness and the assessment of institutional effectiveness are not related. [*Because teaching and learning are fundamental missions of every institution of higher education, the assessment of educational effectiveness is a major component of the assessment of institutional effectiveness.*]

Appendix 5

Department/Program Student Outcomes Survey

1. Does your department require a Capstone/Senior Culminating Experience? ❑ Yes; ❑ No

    If yes, what form does this experience take?

    ❑ A choice among several options *(Check all options available to students)*:

    ❑ Senior Thesis ❑ Topical Seminar ❑ Independent Study
    ❑ Honors Thesis ❑ Service Learning Course ❑ Other
    ❑ Research Seminar ❑ Internship

    ❑ A single course or requirement that must be completed by all students
    (Check which form this requirement takes):

    ❑ Senior Thesis ❑ Topical Seminar ❑ Independent Study
    ❑ Honors Thesis ❑ Service Learning Course ❑ Student Teaching
    ❑ Research Seminar ❑ Internship ❑ Other

2. Is this a Capstone/Culminating Experience required by
    disciplinary accreditation or for professional certification? ❑ Yes; ❑ No

3. Please give examples of how your department adapts its curricula as a result of student performance
    in capstone experiences.

4. Does your department administer its own surveys or questionnaires
    to current students? ❑ Yes; ❑ No

    If yes, when are these questionnaires or surveys administered? *(Check all that apply.)*

    ❑ First Year ❑ Sophomore Year ❑ Junior Year ❑ Senior Year

    Which of the following kinds of information is gathered on these surveys? *(Check all that apply.)*

    ❑ Graduate school applications ❑ Jobs offered ❑ Leadership activities
    ❑ Graduate school acceptances ❑ Jobs accepted ❑ Satisfaction with the institution
    ❑ Graduate school chosen ❑ Expected salary ❑ Satisfaction with department
    ❑ Career plans ❑ Salary for accepted job ❑ Satisfaction with major
    ❑ Jobs applied for ❑ Community service ❑ Satisfaction with teaching
     activities ❑ Perceptions of how their
     education could have been
     improved
     ❑ Other

5. Please give examples of how your department adapts its curricula as a result of student surveys
    or questionnaires.

6. Does your department administer alumni surveys or questionnaires to graduates? ❑ Yes; ❑ No

   If yes, when are these questionnaires or surveys administered? *(Check all that apply.)*

   ❑ At graduation   ❑ Two years after graduation   ❑ Other
   ❑ One year after graduation ❑ Repeatedly on a regular cycle

   Which of the following kinds of information is gathered on alumni surveys or questionnaires?

   ❑ Alumni contact information   ❑ Community service activities
   ❑ Graduate school applications   ❑ Professional leadership activities
   ❑ Graduate school acceptances   ❑ Retrospective satisfaction with the institution
   ❑ Graduate school chosen   ❑ Retrospective satisfaction with department
   ❑ Career plans   ❑ Retrospective satisfaction with major
   ❑ Jobs applied for   ❑ Retrospective satisfaction with teaching
   ❑ Jobs offered   ❑ Retrospective perceptions of how alumni's
   ❑ Expected salary   education could have been improved
   ❑ Current salary   ❑ Other

7. Please give examples of how your department adapts its curricula as a result of alumni surveys or questionnaires.

8. Outside the context of a senior or alumni survey, does your department keep
   an ongoing database or written record of any of the following student data?   ❑ Yes; ❑ No

   If yes, check all that apply.

   ❑ Graduate school applications   ❑ Jobs applied for   ❑ Salary for accepted job
   ❑ Graduate school acceptances   ❑ Community service activities ❑ Other
   ❑ Career plans   ❑ Leadership activities

9. If your department requires its students to take a comprehensive or exist examination (either created in-house or obtained from an external source), please list the name of this examination and its source.

10. Please give examples of how your department adapts its curricula as a result of comprehensive or exit exams.

11. Students may take professional licensure examinations, professional certification examinations, or graduate entrance examinations (e.g., GRE, MCAT, LSAT, GMAT). Please list the exams of this type that your students are likely to take.

12. a. Does your department keep data on the number of students
        taking these professional licensure examinations, professional
        certification examinations, or GREs?   ❑ Yes; ❑ No

    b. Does your department have access to student scores?   ❑ Yes; ❑ No

13. Can you give an examples of how information about scores on professional licensure examinations, professional certification examinations, or GREs are used to adapt your curriculum? Please add an addendum if necessary.

14. Does your department collect student portfolios?   ❏ Yes;   ❏ No

     If yes, are they collected from: ❏ All students   ❏ A random sample

     If your department uses portfolios, briefly describe the types of material included in them. Please add an addendum if necessary.

15. Can you give examples of how your department adapts its curricula as a result of information from student portfolios?

16. Does your department keep an ongoing record of student accomplishments (e.g., student presentations at conferences, student gallery showings of artwork, student publications, student productions, etc.)?   ❏ Yes;   ❏ No

17. Does your department keep an ongoing record of student/faculty collaborative research and scholarship (e.g., presentations, publications, etc.)?   ❏ Yes;   ❏ No

18. Does your department require students to present their work to an audience of their peers and/or faculty?   ❏ Yes;   ❏ No

     If yes, list the course(s) for which such a presentation is required.

19. Does your department keep a record of competitive scholarships, fellowships, internships, or grants awarded to or won by your students?   ❏ Yes;   ❏ No

20. Does your department assess achievement of the general education goals within your program?   ❏ Yes;   ❏ No

     If yes, list the goals you assess, and briefly describe how they are assessed. Please add an addendum if necessary.

21. Can you identify other information-gathering techniques, not listed in this survey, that you use to assess student learning at the department or program level? Please add an addendum if necessary.

22. Which techniques for assessing student learning at the program or departmental level do your faculty find most useful and informative? Please add an addendum if necessary.

Source: The College of New Jersey, Ewing, NJ. Reproduced and adapted with permission.

Appendix 6

Learning Goals and Assessment Techniques

This worksheet can help faculty and staff begin to define important learning goals and to determine appropriate assessment techniques.

	A Important Goals: What students can do after completing the program (course, activity)	B How do students learn to do this?	C What information or evidence is there that students are learning this?	D How has this information been used to help students learn?	E What additional evidence is needed to understand how well students are learning this?	F What possible new or improved assessment tools or techniques might be used?
1.						
2.						
3.						

Appendix 7

From Effect to Cause: A Brainstorming Exercise

The scenarios presented here can be used as the focus of a brainstorming exercise to help faculty and staff members get a sense of the kinds of changes in curriculum and practice that may result from assessment.

Scenario 1. Faculty in the Biophysics Department agree that student majors should be able to make effective oral presentations of their research findings, but they are not satisfied with the quality of the oral presentations made by their seniors. Unfortunately, they can't find a place in the curriculum for students to practice preparing and making oral presentations. All the faculty agree that they have so much content to cover in their courses that they don't have time to teach students how to make effective oral presentations and then listen to them. How might the faculty address this?

Scenario 2. Senior Biology majors at Roselyn College scored poorly on the botany section of the XYZ National Biology Test. Some faculty believe that this is not a concern, because virtually all Roselyn Biology graduates go on to careers in the health and medical fields. Others believe that a grounding in botany is essential to being a well-rounded biologist. How might the faculty resolve this?

Scenario 3. In blind reviews, 85% of Cultural Anthropology senior theses were scored "outstanding" in terms of clarity, organization, the comprehensiveness of their review of scholarly literature, and the soundness of their analysis and conclusions. Five percent were scored "very good," 5% "adequate," and 5% "inadequate." How might the faculty use this information?

Scenario 4. The faculty members of the European Studies Department agree that their student majors should be able to summarize the principles or teachings of the major ancient Greek philosophers. Unfortunately, a review of a sample of student papers shows that the students are generally poor at doing this. To make matters worse, there is only one course in the department that covers ancient Greek philosophy, taught by a senior faculty member who adamantly refuses to consider modifying what or how he teaches. What might the department do?

Scenario 5. One of the goals of the Organizational Leadership program is that students are able to "write clearly and effectively." Although Organizational Leadership majors are asked to write term papers in at least six department courses, their writing quality is nonetheless inadequate by the time they become seniors. Faculty are quick to point to the woefully poor writing skills of entering freshmen and equally quick to blame the English Department for not bringing students' writing skills up to par in freshman composition classes. What, if anything, might be done to improve students' writing skills before they graduate?

Student Learning Styles: Frequently Asked Questions

What is "learning style"?

There is no one universally-accepted definition of the term learning style, but the most frequently cited definition appears to be cognitive, affective, and physiological factors that affect how learners perceive, interact with, and respond to the learning environment (Keefe, 1979).

What is the predominant conception of learning style?

There are many models and instruments for categorizing learning styles, but they have not yet been integrated into an overall learning style theory (Bonham, 1988a; Rayner & Riding, 1997). As Vincent and Ross (2001) note, "Professional educators…are unable to form a consensus regarding the establishment of a single set of accepted principles." Instruments have been developed from at least six models:

1. Field dependence/field independence (Group Embedded Figures Test)

2. Jungian models (Myers-Briggs Type Indicator, Gregorc Style Delineator, Keirsey Temperament Sorter II, Kolb Learning Style Inventory)

3. Sensory (visual-auditory-kinesthetic) models (several inventories)

4. Social interaction models (Grasha-Reichmann Student Learning Style Scales and Learning Preference Scales)

5. Howard Gardner's multiple intelligences model (several inventories)

6. John Biggs' approaches to learning model (Study Process Questionnaire)

These models are not mutually exclusive or necessarily complementary (Vincent & Ross, 2001). The field dependence/field independence model, for example, is similar to the Jungian sensing-intuition scale, and the social interaction models are similar to the Jungian introversion-extroversion scale.

Some instruments (Index of Learning Styles, Productivity Environmental Preference Survey, and some of the instruments listed above) draw on multiple models.

Is the concept of learning style valid and useful?

Vincent and Ross (2001) note that most professional educators "agree that learning styles exist and acknowledge the significant effect that learning styles have on the learning process." The concept of learning styles makes sense intuitively. It is apparent, for example, that some people prefer reading books rather than listening to them on tape and vice versa, and that some people prefer working alone rather than working with others and vice versa (Curry, 1987). Indeed, some learning preferences (e.g., a preference for a quiet background) seem so self-evident that it may not be necessary to have a validated instrument to assess those preferences. As Nagy (1995) notes, "Little can be said about preference questions that ask, for example, what time of day a student prefers to study, except to wonder if such information requires the expense of a standardized test."

Learning style advocates point to a number of validating studies. Swanson (1995), for example, cites numerous studies identifying cultural differences in learning styles, and the discussions of individual instruments that follow include other examples of validating studies.

Critics, however, point out that for a learning style theory to be valid and useful, it must be shown that students learn more effectively when their learning styles are accommodated, and only a limited number of studies have shown this. Some therefore feel that the usefulness or validity of learning style models and instruments has not been definitively established (Bonham, 1988a; Bonham, 1988b; Kavale & Forness, 1987; Rayner & Riding, 1997).

While unvalidated instruments should not be used to make potentially harmful decisions about students, pedagogy, curriculum, etc., they may be used to help students gain self-awareness, provided that students have the opportunity to complete several instruments, so they do not take the results of any one instrument too seriously.

A particular concern (Grasha, 1990; Stellwagen, 2001) is that most learning style theories label or pigeonhole students into a few discrete, quantitative, often dichotomous categories, rather than recognizing that individuals develop and practice a qualitative mixture of learning styles that evolve as they learn and grow and that vary by discipline (Silver, Strong, & Perini, 1997). In some instances, pigeonholing begets a risk of stereotyping cultural groups.

How can faculty members use information on learning styles to help students learn?

Faculty members first should understand that students use a variety of approaches to learning that may not match their own. Schroeder (1993) reports that over 75% of faculty members prefer the Myers-Briggs intuitive style and learn best through abstract concepts, ideas, and theories, compared to just 40% of entering students and 25% of the general population. Most students, in contrast, prefer the sensing style and learn best through concrete, practical, structured, and sequential experiences.

Anderson and Adams (1992) and Wilson (1998) urge faculty members to use a flexible variety of approaches to help students learn; Montgomery and Groat (2002), and Vincent and Ross (2001) offer specific suggestions. In addition to offering the usual lectures and readings, faculty can engage their students' senses and give them an idea of structure by providing visual aids such as bulleted lists, charts, and diagrams; written outlines or study guides of key points; structured opportunities for group interaction; practical "real world" examples;

and a variety of assignment formats. They can also try to get to know their students, help their students get to know them, and provide plenty of feedback. Most good teachers, of course, already do this instinctively.

Claxton and Murrell (1987) further recommend that faculty members:

1. Participate in workshops and other professional development opportunities that help them better understand the importance of learning style and its role in improving students' learning.

2. Engage in classroom research that investigates how information on learning styles can improve their teaching.

3. Create curricular experiences that help students learn how to learn by raising their awareness of their own preferences and strengths and developing strategies for succeeding in courses taught by faculty members whose styles differ from their own.

Should faculty members aim to accommodate each student's learning style?

Faculty members should not try to accommodate individual learning styles for several reasons.

1. Models of teaching and learning styles are not yet sufficiently validated to be able to determine definitively how each student learns best and customize instruction accordingly (Zarghani, 1988).

2. As Gregorc (cited in Wilson, 1998) notes, "attempting to teach to all students' styles can quickly cause a teacher to burn out." Gardner (1996) states that "there is no point in assuming that every topic can be effectively approached in at least seven ways, and it is a waste of effort and time to attempt to do this."

3. While students should use their "strong" learning styles to best advantage, it's just as appropriate for them to develop their abilities to use other learning styles (Grasha, 1990; Montgomery & Groat, 2002) and to work with faculty whose styles differ from their own.

How might students learn about their own learning styles?

Because any one instrument is an incomplete, imperfect assessment of learning style, students should not let any one instrument dictate their learning styles (Bonham, 1988a). Instead, they should be encouraged to develop their own sense of their learning styles, using multiple learning style inventories as clues rather than as definitive determinations. Crowe (2000) and Grasha (1990) suggest that students could be asked to:

❑ Write a paragraph or two explaining how they learn best.

❑ Complete at least two learning style inventories (perhaps chosen from among the Keirsey Temperament Sorter, the VARK Questionnaire, Owens and Barnes' Learning Preference Scales, the Multiple Intelligences Developmental Assessment Scales, and the Study Process Questionnaire) and compare the results with their self-description.

❑ After completing a course project, write a reflection on what and how they learned from the project.

❑ Use all of the above to develop a refined statement of how they learn best, along with a list of study/learning strategies they could use to take best advantage of their own particular learning style and to help them learn in situations where they must use approaches that do not correspond with their style.

References

Anderson, J. A. (2001). Developing a learning/teaching style assessment model for diverse populations. In Linda Suskie (Ed.), *Assessment to promote deep learning: Insight from AAHE's 2000 and 1999 Assessment Conferences*. Washington: American Association for Higher Education.

Anderson, J. A., & Adams, M. (1992). Acknowledging the learning styles of diverse student populations: Implications for instructional design. In L. L. B. Border & N. V. Chism (Eds.), *Teaching for diversity*. San Francisco: Jossey-Bass.

Bonham, L. A. (1988a). Learning style use: In need of perspective. *Lifelong Learning: An Omnibus of Practice and Research, 11*(5), 14-17, 19.

Bonham, L. A. (1988b). Learning style instruments: *Let the buyer beware. Lifelong Learning: An Omnibus of Practice and Research, 11* (6), 12-16.

Claxton, D. S., & Murrell, P. (1987). *Learning styles: Implications for improving educational practices* (Report No. 4). Washington: Association for the Study of Higher Education.

Cornwell, J. M., & Manfredo, P. A. (1994, Summer). Kolb's learning style theory revisited. *Educational & Psychological Measurement, 54* (2), 317-328.

Crowe, R. (2000). *Know your student's learning style: The missing link in the lecture v. active learning issue*. Paper presented at the NISOD Conference, Austin, TX.

Curry, L. (1987). *Integrating concepts of cognitive or learning style: A review with attention to psychometric standards*. Ottawa: Canadian College of Health Service Executives.

Dunn, R., & Griggs, S. (1995). A meta-analytic validation of the Dunn and Dunn model of learning-style preferences. *Journal of Educational Research, 88* (6), 353-362.

Gardner, H. (1996, Apr.). Multiple intelligences: Myths and messages. *International Schools Journal, 15* (2), 8-22.

Grasha, T. (1990). The naturalistic approach to learning styles. *College Teaching, 38* (3), 106-114.

Hayes, J. & Allinson, C. W. (1997, May-June). Learning styles and training and development in work. *Educational Psychology, 17* (1/2), 185-194.

Kavale, K. & Forness, S. (1987). Style over substance: Assessing the effectiveness of modality testing and teaching. *Exceptional Children*, 54, 228-239.

Kavale, K. A., Hirshoren, A., & Forness, S. R. (1998, Spring). Meta-analytic validation of the Dunn and Dunn model of learning-style preferences: A critique of what was Dunn. *Learning Disabilities Research and Practice, 13* (2), 75-80.

Keefe, J. W. (Ed.) (1979). *Student learning styles: Diagnosing and prescribing programs*. Reston, VA: National Association of Secondary School Principals.

Klein, P. D. (1997, Fall). Multiplying the problems of intelligence by eight: A critique of Gardner's theory. *Canadian Journal of Education, 22* (4), 377-394.

Lewthwaite, B., & Dunham, P. H. (1999). *Enriching teaching scholarship through learning styles*. Paper presented at the Annual Meeting of the American Association of Colleges for Teacher Education, Washington.

Montgomery, S. M., & Groat, L. N. (2002). *Student learning styles and their implications for teaching*. Ann Arbor: Center for Research on Learning and Teaching, University of Michigan.

Nagy, P. (1995). Review of the Learning Style Profile. In J. C. Conoley & J. C. Impara (Eds.), *The Twelfth Mental Measurements Yearbook*. Lincoln, NE: Buros Institute of Mental Measurements.

O'Neil, J. (1990). Making sense of style. *Educational Leadership, 48* (2), 4-9.

Presland, J. (1994). Learning styles and continuous professional development. *Educational Psychology in Practice, 10*, 179-184.

Rayner, S. & Riding, R. (1997). Towards a categorization of cognitive styles and learning styles. *Educational Psychology, 17* (1/2), 5-29.

Ruble, T. L., & Stout, D. E. *A critical assessment of Kolb's learning style inventory*. ERIC Document Reproduction Service No. ED 377221.

Rule, D. L., & Grippin, P. C. (1988). *A critical comparison of learning style instruments frequently used with adult learners*. Paper presented at the Annual Conference of the Eastern Educational Research Association, Miami Beach.

Schroeder, C. C. (1993, Sept./Oct.) New students – New learning styles. *Change*.

Seidel, L. E., & England, E. M. (1997). *Gregorc's cognitive styles: Preference for instructional and assessment techniques in college students*. Poster presented at the Annual Convention of the American Psychological Society, Washington.

Sewall, T. J. (1986). *The measurement of learning style: A critique of four assessment tools*. University of Wisconsin at Green Bay, Assessment Center. ERIC Document Reproduction Service No. ED 267247.

Shearer, B. (n.d.). *Assessment of the multiple intelligences: Theoretical issues*. Multiple Intelligences Special Interest Group of the American Educational Research Association. Available online: http://www.geocities.com/Athens/Column/7568/assessment.htm.

Silver, H., Strong, R., & Perini, M. (1997, Sept.) Integrating learning styles and multiple intelligences. *Educational Leadership, 55* (1), 22-27.

Stellwagen, J. B. (2001, May/June). A challenge to the learning style advocates. *Clearing House, 74* (5), 265-269.

Swanson, L. J. (1995, July). *Learning styles: A review of the literature*. The Claremont Graduate School. ERIC Document Reproduction Service No. ED 387067.

Thompson, P., et al. (1979, April). *Interrelationships among five cognitive style tests, student characteristics, and achievement*. Paper presented at the Annual Meeting of the American Educational Research Association, San Francisco. ERIC Document Reproduction Service No. ED 174678.

Traub, J. (1998, October 26). Multiple intelligence disorder. *The New Republic*.

Vincent, A., & Ross, D. (2001, Summer). Learning style awareness: A basis for developing teaching and learning strategies. *Journal of Research on Technology in Education, 33* (5).

Wilson, V. A. (1998, Jan. 1). *Learning how they learn: A review of the literature on learning styles*. Muskingum College. ERIC Document Reproduction Service No. ED 427017.

Zarghani, G. H. Z. (1988). *Identification of learning style strategies which enable college students with differing personality temperament to cope with learning blocks*. Unpublished doctoral dissertation, University of Nebraska, Lincoln.

References

Anastasi, A. & Urbina, S. (1996). *Psychological Testing, Seventh Edition*. Upper Saddle River, NJ :Prentice-Hall.

Angelo, T. A. & Cross, P. K. (1993). *Classroom assessment techniques: A handbook for college teachers* (2nd ed.). San Francisco: Jossey-Bass.

Angelo, T. A., Ewell, P.T., & Lopez, C. (2001). *Assessment at the millennium: Now what?* In L. Suskie (Ed.), *Assessment to Promote Deep Learning* (pp. 59-63). Washington, DC: American Association for Higher Education.

Association of College & Research Libraries. (2000). *Information literacy competency standards for higher education*. Chicago: Author.

Astin, A. (1991). *Assessment for excellence: The philosophy and practice of assessment and evaluation in higher education*. Portland: Oryx Press and the American Council on Education.

Banta, T. W., Lund, J. P., Black, K. E., & Oblander, F. W. (1996). *Assessment in practice: Putting principles to work on college campuses*. San Francisco: Jossey-Bass.

Briggs-Myers, I. & McCaulley, M. (1992). *Manual and guide to the use of the Myers-Briggs Type Indicator*. Consulting Psychologists Press.

Chickering, A. & Gamson, Z. F. (1991). Applying the seven principles for good practice in higher education. *New Directions for Teaching and Learning, No. 47*. San Francisco: Jossey-Bass.

Gall, J. P., Borg, W. R. & Gall, M. D. (1998). *Applying educational research: A practical guide* (4th ed.). Boston: Allyn & Bacon.

Gardner, H. (1983). *Frames of mind: The theory of multiple intelligences*. New York: Basic Books.

Haladyna, T. M. (1999). *Developing and validation multiple choice test items*. Mahwah, NJ: Erlbaum.

Hartman, V. F. (1995). Teaching and learning style preferences: Transitions through technology. *VCCA Journal, 9*, 2, 18-20.

Huba, M. E. & Freed, J. E. (2000). *Learner-centered assessment on college campuses*. Needham Heights: Allyn & Bacon.

Kolb, D. A. (1984). *Experiential learning: Experience as the source of learning and development*. Hillsdale, NJ: Prentice Hall.

Krueger, R. A. & Casey, M. A. (2000). *Focus groups: A practical guide for applied research*. London: Sage.

Maxwell, J. A. A. (1996). *Qualitative research design: An interactive approach*. London: Sage.

Middle States Commission on Higher Education. (2002). *Characteristics of excellence in higher education: Eligibility requirements and standards for accreditation*. Philadelphia: Author.

_____. (2003). *Developing research and communication skills: Guidelines for information literacy in the curriculum*. Philadelphia: Author.

Morgan, D. L. (1997). *Focus Groups As Qualitative Research, Second Edition*. London: Sage.

Palomba, C. A. & Banta, T. W. (1999). *Assessment essentials: Planning, implementing, improving*. San Francisco: Jossey-Bass.

Pascarella, E. T. & Terenzini, P. T. (1991). *How college affects students: Findings and insights from twenty years of research*. San Francisco: Jossey-Bass.

Schein, E. (1996). *Organizational culture and leadership*. San Francisco: Jossey-Bass.

Silverman, D. J. (2001). *Interpreting qualitative data: Methods for analyzing talk, text and interaction.* (2nd ed.). London: Sage

Sternberg, R. J. (1988). *The triarchic mind: A new theory of human intelligence.* New York: Viking Press.

Stufflebeam, D. L. (2001). Evaluation models. *New Directions for Evaluation, No. 89.* San Francisco: Jossey-Bass.

Suskie, L. (1996). *Questionnaire survey research: What works?* (2nd ed.). Tallahassee, Florida: Association for Institutional Research.

Walvoord, B. E. & Anderson, V. J. (1998). *Effective grading: A tool for learning and assessment.* San Francisco: Jossey-Bass.